INTERIOR
STYLE
coastal

JENA QUINN &
LUCY DERBYSHIRE

contents

Coastal interior design captures the essence of seaside living, seamlessly blending natural elements and soothing colours to create spaces that evoke the tranquillity and beauty of the landscape. The radiant luminosity and the enchanting oceanic palette seamlessly merge in interiors, bridging the gap between indoor and outdoor living. This captivating aesthetic comes to life through the artful curation of natural materials, from the inviting embrace of rattan furniture to the timeless allure of timber panelling, all complemented by airy fresh linen and white paint.

The book begins with a historical exploration of the decorating style's evolution, paying homage to the cultural influences and visionary pioneers who have shaped this distinctive genre. We traverse from the French Riviera to the East and West coasts of the United States, showcasing iconic interiors that pioneered the coastal vernacular.

The second section of the book celebrates the diversity of the décor, showcasing exemplary examples that embody various interpretations of the aesthetic. Within these pages, we applaud individual creativity rooted in shared coastal design principles.

The final section delves deeper into these design principles, offering a professional interior design perspective on skilfully infusing coastal charm into your own home. We unlock the secrets of coastal interiors and guide you in transforming your living spaces into serene retreats.

previous page *The beach house of fashion designer Donna Karan in Parrot Cay, Turks and Caicos Islands, with architecture by Cheong Yew Kuan and interior design by Enrico Bonetti and Dominic Kozerski.*

right *The Butterfly House, a mid-century modern home with a unique winged roof to take advantage of the view, overlooks the Big Sur coastline in Carmel-by-the-Sea, California. It was designed by architect Francis W. Wynkoop in 1951, with the interior renovated by Jamie Bush and Co. in 2018.*

The coast has not always held the allure of idyllic escapism that we associate with it today. Throughout antiquity and up until the eighteenth century, the coastal landscape was an inhospitable frontier, a dangerous wilderness. However, as the nineteenth century dawned, a remarkable transformation took place. The stark contrast between the once perilous coastline and the emerging concept of escapism and enjoyment began to unfold, giving rise to a new perception that would shape the course of coastal history.

A new appreciation for the healing powers of fresh air, exercise and sea water saw coastal communities flourishing to cater to a growing clientele, seeking health and hygiene benefits. Doctors began prescribing 'sea air' and 'salt water', leading to a common practice of seasonal migration to beachside resorts for medical treatment. The coastline evolved into a retreat from modernity, symbolizing health and pleasure, where

history

individuals sought refuge from the strains of daily life. Significant technological advancements in transportation, such as the expansion of passenger sea travel and improved road networks, rendered coastal settlements increasingly accessible to people from all walks of life. What was once considered a luxury exclusive to the elite became attainable for the middle classes as well. From the French Riviera to the East and West Coasts of the United States, coastal architecture and interiors have always been influenced by the beauty and expansiveness of the sea.

opposite *The house of film producer Albert Lewin in Santa Monica, California, was designed by modernist architects Richard Neutra and Peter Pfisterer in 1938 and became the home of actress Mae West in 1954.*

The French Riviera

This period in history from the late nineteenth century to the outbreak of World War I stands as a time of remarkable tranquillity, economic prosperity and cultural blossoming. Fondly remembered as the Belle Époque, which translates as 'Beautiful Era', it was characterized by grandeur and elegance, with the aristocracy and high society playing prominent roles in shaping the cultural landscape. Extravagant parties, luxurious lifestyles and opulent arts patronage were hallmarks of this elite class. Their influence extended beyond cultural pursuits as they often played vital roles in politics and diplomacy, contributing to the era's political stability.

A beautiful architectural expression of the time can be found in Villa Kérylos, located in Beaulieu-sur-Mer, built between 1902–8. The house is surrounded on three sides by the crystal waters of the Mediterranean Sea, with an impressive backdrop of the mountains of Èze and panoramic views of the harbour.

Beyond its inherent aesthetic charm, Villa Kérylos perfectly encapsulates the spirit of the Belle Époque, symbolizing the yearning to recreate and revive the timeless beauty and wisdom of ancient Greek civilization. It reflects a deep appreciation for the values and ideals of classical antiquity, serving as a place of intellectual exchange and cultural enlightenment.

The grandeur and opulence of Villa Kérylos stand as a testament to the intellectual curiosity and artistic flair of the Belle Époque era. Conceived by French archaeologist and mathematician Théodore Reinach (1860–1928), the villa was not a mere imitation of ancient Greece, but a thoughtful reinvention that skilfully blended influences from Rome, Pompeii and Egypt. Designed by the talented architect Emmanuel Pontremoli (1865–1956), Villa Kérylos seamlessly fused philhellenism, 'the love of Greek culture', with modern amenities, creating a timeless and elegant ambiance that embraced the prevailing trends of the time.

above *The drawing room of Villa Kérylos with windows looking into the courtyard. Frescoes, furniture and mosaics were based on Greek antiquities and portray deities and heroes.*

above *On the external walls of Villa Kérylos, windows open to the Mediterranean Sea, letting in light and allowing an unrestricted view.*

Stepping inside the villa, one is transported to a world of romanticized reflection from a golden age of art and culture. The open central atrium and courtyard, lined with Carrara marble columns, harked back to Greek architectural traditions, allowing natural light to flood the interior and fostering a sense of connectivity with the surrounding landscape. This design element, which would later become prevalent in the modernist movement, showcased the forward-thinking approach of the villa's creators.

The interior spaces of Villa Kérylos were meticulously planned, with a focus on symmetry and proportion, reflecting classical ideals. Traditional materials of ancient Greece, such as stucco, Carrara marble, stone and terracotta, were carefully employed to establish a faithful recreation of Greek design principles, further enhancing the building's timeless allure.

Every surface within the villa received an exceptional level of attention to detail, from the mosaics on the floor to the frescoes on the walls and the hand-painted wooden beams of the ceiling. The layers of texture and decorative motifs depicting scenes from Greek mythology created a striking and unique impact that was both awe-inspiring and utterly breathtaking.

Authenticity was the cornerstone of Villa Kérylos's interior success, extending even to the furniture design and accessories. Reinach commissioned exact replicas of ancient Grecian furniture from the National Archaeological Museum in Naples, complemented by original designs from Pontremoli. Crafted from rare exotic woods, these furniture pieces enhanced the overall decorative richness that Reinach sought to achieve.

The villa's lavish interiors, artistic detailing and stunning panoramic views reflect the economic prosperity of the Belle Époque era and serve as a testament to the wealth and sophistication of its owner, Théodore Reinach. Villa Kérylos exemplifies the opulent style of architecture and design that became a defining characteristic of the Belle Époque period, with grand buildings along the coastline becoming symbols of wealth and social standing.

Another striking example of a palatial mansion along the coastline during the era is Villa Rothschild, also known as Villa Ephrussi de Rothschild, located in Saint-Jean-Cap-Ferrat. Built between 1905 and 1912 for Béatrice Ephrussi de Rothschild, a distinguished member of two influential families — the Rothschilds and the Ephrussis — it serves as a true reflection of the extravagant tastes of the Belle Époque.

The Ephrussi family, of Austrian-Jewish descent, was renowned for their vast wealth and social prominence in the late nineteenth and early twentieth centuries. Béatrice in particular was a remarkable figure, known not only for her lavish lifestyle but also for her cultural and artistic contributions. The family art collection was beautifully captured in Edmund de Waal's extraordinary history of a family through 264 objects, *The Hare with Amber Eyes*.

The villa's design is an eclectic blend of architectural styles, showcasing the period's love for mixing influences. Renaissance, Spanish and Italian elements come together harmoniously to create a visually stunning exterior, symbolizing the cultural richness and cosmopolitanism of the time. Inside, visitors are greeted with luxurious and sumptuous interiors reminiscent of Villa Kérylos. Lavish materials such as marble, precious woods and intricate stucco work adorn the spaces, each applied with meticulous attention to detail. Opulent furnishings, dazzling chandeliers and an exquisite art collection all speak of the owner's immense wealth and refined taste, mirroring the lifestyle of the Belle Époque elite.

One of the notable features of the villa is its diverse themed rooms. Each room represents a specific cultural and artistic style, curated to showcase different aspects of beauty and creativity. This amalgamation of styles results in a visually stimulating interior, where luxury meets fascination.

The carefully crafted interior served as an exciting backdrop for entertaining guests and displaying the refined tastes and artistic inclinations of high society. This was especially significant during a time when the rising middle

above *The apartments of Baroness Béatrice at the Villa Rothschild on Saint-Jean-Cap-Ferrat open out to colonnades, gardens and the Mediterranean beyond.*

classes, known as the 'bourgeoisie', gained significant wealth and social influence. They sought to flaunt their newfound prosperity through luxurious homes, fashionable attire and extravagant social events.

Given that the French Riviera was a favoured destination for the wealthy and elite during this period, the houses along the coastline needed to epitomize a lifestyle of luxury and excess. They became a stage for lavish parties, elaborate dinners and grand soirées, providing the elite with opportunities to showcase their wealth and social standing.

Villa Rothschild, with its grandeur and allure, soon became one of the central hubs for the vibrant social life of the Belle Époque. It stood as a testament to the magnificence of the era, where coastal interiors played a significant role in defining the extravagant lifestyle and aspirations of the upper classes.

above *The swimming pool at the Château de l'Horizon links the interior of the château with the sea beyond. To the left is the legendary water slide.*

The French Riviera became a magnetic draw for British, European and American aristocracy seeking to bask in its glorious climate and indulge in an extravagant lifestyle. As the rich and famous flocked to the region, the humble dwellings of the local fishing community underwent an irrevocable transformation. The once-serene coast was now infused with glitz and glamour, echoing the opulent aspirations of the era's society.

As for the elite, their seaside visits went beyond mere pursuits of health or relaxation; they were also about showcasing their social standing. The coast became a stage for the wealthy to be seen, a platform to display their refined tastes and extravagant lifestyles. Seaside attire and lavish social gatherings at specific locations became part of the cultural norm, turning the French Riviera into a hub of society's most captivating events.

Another pinnacle location for the notorious gatherings of high society during the Belle Époque was the modernist villa, Château de l'Horizon, where the parties became legendary. This architectural marvel, often referred to as the White Palace on the Water, holds historical significance not only for its stunning design but also for the distinguished guests who graced its halls before and after the war. Among them were the Duke and Duchess of Windsor, Sir Winston Churchill, Marilyn Monroe, Noël Coward, Elizabeth Taylor and many other luminaries of the era. The villa's reputation was built on its extravagant dinner parties and social gatherings, attracting celebrities such as Greta Garbo, Jack L. Warner and Maurice Chevalier for decades.

Constructed in 1932 by the celebrated American architect of the modernist movement Barry Dierks (1899–1960), Château de l'Horizon was commissioned by Maxine Elliott. The enchanting actress and consummate hostess was renowned for her boundless hospitality, regularly hosting lunches for 50 guests and holding continuous pool parties, where her guests could glide down a water slide into the sea, promoting cultural dynamism and carefree enjoyment.

Dierks' brilliant design was aimed at optimizing the villa's stunning view of the Mediterranean Sea while seamlessly connecting the interior with the surrounding landscape. The château stands as a testament to the experimentation and artistic expression of the era, incorporating elements from various architectural styles and embodying the spirit of innovation and individuality. These very qualities would later become key elements of the modernist movement, an architectural movement that took hold in the French Riviera during the 1930s.

Château de l'Horizon stands as a symbol of the Belle Époque's opulence and extravagance, immortalizing the grandeur of an era defined by social gatherings, artistic expression and architectural innovation. The house's reputation for lavishness made it a particularly fitting setting for actress Rita Hayworth's iconic wedding celebration with the château's new owner, Prince Ali Khan, where the swimming pool was filled with 200 gallons of eau de cologne and topped with the couple's initials made from flowers. According to *LIFE* magazine, 'it smelled very nice', as the guests were treated to 50 pounds of caviar and 600 bottles of champagne. This event further solidified the château's status as a symbol of luxury and decadence. Its historical significance and association with some of the most celebrated figures of the time continue to captivate the imagination, making it a timeless testament to the cultural dynamism of the French Riviera in the early twentieth century.

During this era, a new architectural ethos began to emerge, shifting the focus toward the internal experience as the driving force of design. The principle of 'form follows function' became paramount, with the exterior appearance of buildings being a direct product of their intended interior use. This architectural approach came to be known as the modernist movement, which emphasized the importance of simplicity and functionality.

Prominent architects of the day, such as Le Corbusier (1887–1965) and Walter Gropius (1883–1969), promoted the modernist doctrine in Europe. They advocated for large expanses of glass, minimal ornamentation, cantilevered balconies, the use of white concrete, flat roofs and strong geometrical shapes. The incorporation of extensive windows, glass doors and skylights allowed natural light to flood the interior spaces, blurring the lines between indoors and outdoors. This integration of the surrounding landscape became an integral part of the architectural experience.

Open floor plans became a hallmark of modernist design, fostering a sense of space and connectivity between rooms. This arrangement not only improved the quality of light and ventilation throughout the house but also enhanced the overall spatial experience.

opposite *The interior of Villa Noailles in Hyères, an example of a cubist interior with integrated spaces over many levels.*

overleaf *Eileen Gray's modernist masterpiece and example of indoor/outdoor living, E-1027 embraced floor-to-ceiling windows and open-plan spaces.*

In contrast to earlier architectural styles, which favoured ornate decorative elements, modernist design was characterized by minimalism. The ethos dictated that every element of the design should serve a functional purpose, with no room for superfluous ornamentation. This allowed the purity of the building's form and the fundamental materials to take centre stage, devoid of distractions.

The new attention to the purity of form was directly inspired by cubism, a movement pioneered by Pablo Picasso (1881–1973) and Georges Braque (1882–1963), during the twentieth century. While cubism was primarily an art movement centred around painting, the innovative approach to form, space and multiple perspectives had a profound impact on architectural design at the time. Contemporary architects drew inspiration from the cubist principles and applied them to modern architecture, which shaped the aesthetics and spatial experience of buildings throughout the twentieth century. Cubism's characteristic fragmentation of forms, where objects were broken down into geometric shapes and planes, influenced modernist architects to experiment with fragmented and abstracted façades. Buildings began to feature irregular and angular shapes, departing from the traditional façades seen in earlier architecture. In cubist art, objects were simultaneously depicted from multiple viewpoints, leading to the concept of 'simultaneity'. In architecture, this translated into designs that allowed occupants to experience and view spaces from various angles. Buildings with open floor plans, interconnected spaces and large windows were created to provide dynamic and ever-changing perspectives. Cubism's emphasis on transparent planes and overlapping forms inspired architects to explore concepts of transparency. Glass façades, curtain walls and open structures allowed light to filter through spaces, creating a sense of visual layering and depth.

Through the focus of simplicity of form, modernist architects began exploring and embracing new materials and construction techniques. They started working with reinforced concrete, steel and large glass panes, all offering new opportunities and possibilities within the realms of construction while representing the spirit of innovation of the era. Through concrete, structures became much stronger and more resilient, resulting in taller buildings, longer spans without supports and more daring architectural forms. Steel frames meant that buildings no longer had to rely solely on load-bearing walls, facilitating larger windows and more open floor plans, transforming interior design as we know it. Advances in glass technology pioneered the creation of larger panes and the birth of the curtain wall. All these advancements played a crucial role in shaping the architectural landscape of the twentieth century and through pushing the boundaries of what was possible, architectural innovation was discovered.

Artists, writers, celebrities and intellectuals were naturally drawn to the free-spirited modernist movement. This was mainly in response to the location of the French Riviera, where the movement was pioneered. Stunning views and natural beauty combined with the new cultural dynamism fostered an environment conducive to architectural experimentation and innovation. The elite clientele often had progressive tastes, which would in turn push architects and designers to be at the forefront of the modernist movement.

One of the most iconic examples of the modernist movement is the renowned hamlet of Cap Moderne, nestled near Monaco in the picturesque village of Roquebrune-Cap-Martin. This extraordinary site offers a rare and fascinating glimpse into the minds of two of the twentieth century's most influential architects, Eileen Gray (1878–1976) and Le Corbusier, and the modernist movement to which they were integral.

Today, it stands as one of the greatest and most exceptional collections of modernist architecture, providing a rich reference point for contemporary designers and enthusiasts alike.

E-1027, the iconic masterpiece designed between 1926 and 1929 by the Irish designer Eileen Gray and her architect lover, Jean Badovici (1893–1956), stands as the epitome of the pioneering theories of the modernist movement. The villa features a simple geometric cube supported on stilts, boasting oversized windows and an open-plan living room. Its design bears a striking ocean-liner aesthetic:

long and narrow, yet commanding an enormous presence despite its modest proportions.

The interior of E-1027 is as remarkable as its architecture, reflecting Gray's innovative ideas in living spaces and her keen eye for functional yet elegant design. The fluid open floor plan showcases her belief in multifunctional spaces, easily adaptable to the needs of the inhabitants. She meticulously designed freestanding furniture, lamps and decorations to perfectly suit the open-plan space she created. Her furniture exemplifies practicality and dual functionality, extending the notion of 'form follows function' beyond architecture into furniture design. Cupboards and furnishings blend seamlessly into the house, becoming intrinsic elements of its design.

The attention to detail is evident in every aspect of the interior, from the way light falls on contents to the integration of electrical fittings and radiators. Gray's design includes clever features such as wardrobe doors doubling as privacy screens, adjustable windows to modify airflow and a bathtub with a waterproof curtain to prevent flooding during showers.

Surface materials were carefully chosen to create playful juxtapositions, incorporating modern materials such as glass and steel alongside traditional elements like wood and textiles. This combination gives the interior a modern yet timeless feel. A soothing colour palette, ranging from neutral whites and light pinks to marine greens and indigos, harmonizes with the Mediterranean setting. Gray deliberately chose subtle Mediterranean

colours, evoking the hues of deep water, seashells and sunsets, avoiding clichéd coastal palettes.

Large windows and terraces offer panoramic views of the Mediterranean, allowing the occupants to continuously engage with the surrounding landscape. The seamless transition and connection with nature were masterfully orchestrated, with internal and external spaces designed in harmony.

Gray's philosophy of design, prioritizing functionality without compromising on aesthetics, is evident throughout E-1027's interior. It embodies modernist principles, demonstrating that spaces can be minimal, functional and beautiful all at once. The villa stands as a testament to the brilliance of Eileen Gray and her significant contribution to the modernist movement, leaving a lasting impact on the world of interior design and architecture.

above *The interior of E-1027 was designed by Eileen Gray, including furniture such as her Bibendum chair, seen left. Le Corbusier's murals appear on the far right.*

above *The cantilevered and shuttered windows of E-1027 allowed precise regulation of airflow, and rails allowed the shutters to slide open and closed to regulate sunlight. Gray said, 'A window without shutters is like an eye without eyelids.'*

opposite *Reflective, industrial materials were used in the master bathroom, including a tub covered in aluminium sheeting.*

Following the completion of E-1027 in 1929, Jean Badovici's connection with Thomas Rebutato led to an exciting development near the modernist 'White Villa'. Rebutato acquired the adjacent plot and had ambitious plans to build a small development of six cabins, with five serving as minimalist holiday huts and one for his own use, as well as a bar and restaurant called L'Etoile de Mer. Serendipitously, Badovici and Le Corbusier were the restaurant's first guests, leading to a strong friendship between the two men.

Le Corbusier, a pioneering figure in modern architecture, was already making waves with his groundbreaking ideas and innovative designs, reshaping society's perception of architecture and urban planning. Like Eileen Gray, he was driven by a commitment to functionality, efficiency and the belief in architecture's transformative power to improve people's lives. He aimed to create environments that embraced modernity while enhancing the wellbeing of their occupants. His involvement in the project led to the design of the remaining five cabins, now known as Les Unités de Camping, in exchange for a small piece of land, where he built Le Cabanon for himself.

Through Le Corbusier's contribution, this new cluster of cabins seamlessly integrated into the architectural collection of Cap Martin, creating a congenial whole. Each structure harmoniously complemented the other, reflecting the shared principles of the modernist movement – simplicity, functionality and an appreciation for the transformative potential of design. The synergy between E-1027 and Les Unités de Camping added depth and significance to the architectural landscape, solidifying its reputation as a haven for modernist design and innovation.

Les Unités de Camping are celebrated for their experimental nature, innovative design and their embodiment of Le Corbusier's vision for modern architecture in harmony with nature. Each unit became a canvas for pushing the boundaries of architectural design, allowing Le Corbusier to explore and test

opposite Le Corbusier's Le Cabanon, decorated with his abstract murals, is a colourful contrast to the pristine White Villa nearby.

opposite *The modular and multifunctional interior of Le Cabanon. The floor is painted bright yellow while the ceiling is clad in various panels of green, red, white and black. Pale colours are used to reflect light in daytime spaces while dark colours enhance shadow in sleep areas.*

modern ideas within a real context. Designed as modular structures, they were meant to be easily replicated and adapted to different locations and properties, reflecting the architect's belief in standardization and mass production as a solution to housing shortages and societal challenges of the time.

Despite the challenges posed by the small spaces, Le Corbusier maximized their use by cleverly incorporating multifunctional spaces and interior layouts, making them comfortable and practical holiday retreats. This modest and compact design approach was also evident in Le Cabanon, his own summer cottage built in 1952, located right next to L'Etoile de Mer. The interior of Le Cabanon followed the same modular principles emphasized in his other works. It represented a manifestation of Le Corbusier's architectural principles, showcasing efficient use of space, functional design and a seamless integration of architecture with nature.

Le Cabanon's interior was entirely clad in wood, with a compact space of 15 square metres (162 square feet) incorporating areas for relaxation, work and washing. Furniture was limited to a bed, table and storage, demonstrating the simplicity and efficiency that defined Le Corbusier's approach. The space was illuminated by two small windows, while the yellow floor and green and red ceiling panels aimed to transport the appearance of a primitive hut into a work of art. To further enhance the design, Le Corbusier adorned L'Etoile de Mer and the entrance of Le Cabanon with abstract murals, characteristic of his artistic style.

The abstract and colourful geometric compositions featured in these murals added a dynamic and visually striking element to both buildings, creating an environment that captivated the senses. Le Corbusier's artistry in these murals exemplified his ability to integrate different facets of design, from architecture to painting, into a cohesive and harmonious whole. Together, Les Unités de Camping and Le Cabanon stand as testaments to his profound impact on modern architecture, showcasing innovative ideas, a visionary approach and a deep appreciation of the connection between design and nature.

Despite Le Corbusier's initial outrage at the idea of a woman creating a significant work in what he considered his own style, he was eventually forced to share the accolade of pioneering the modern movement with Eileen Gray. Both designers adopted the same five components – concrete piles, open-plan rooms, roof gardens, horizontal windows and 'free' façades in their work. However, internally, Gray created intimate spaces that slowly revealed themselves to the user, contrasting with the more brightly coloured and expressive exteriors of Le Corbusier's holiday huts and Le Cabanon.

The holiday huts, rendered with vibrant colours, stood in stark contrast to the crisp white cube of E-1027, causing Gray to view them as a form of 'cultural vandalism' to her vision. Le Corbusier's sub-Picasso murals, found throughout the complex, including on Gray's own house, served as a continuous expression of this use of colour. After Gray's separation from Badovici shortly after E-1027's completion, Badovici encouraged Le Corbusier to paint bright murals on the plain white walls. Whether Le Corbusier painted these murals out of admiration for her work or jealousy, he has become an integral part of E-1027's history and the murals became a common thread throughout the mini-complex.

For Eileen Gray, the addition of these murals was seen as a violation of her design principles. Despite the initial tensions, both Gray and Le Corbusier's contributions to the Cap Moderne complex showcase the richness and diversity within the modern movement. Their works demonstrate the dynamic and ever-evolving nature of architectural design during this period, with each designer adding their own unique flair and vision to the architectural landscape. The juxtaposition of styles, while contentious at times, contributed to the legacy of Cap Moderne as an extraordinary collection of modernist architecture, capturing the spirit of innovation and experimentation of the early twentieth century.

right *Gray's E-1027 in the foreground on Cap Martin, with Le Corbusier's holiday huts sited behind.*

opposite *The interior of Villa Santo Sospir displays the frescoes of Jean Cocteau, as well as his Aubusson tapestry hung on the wall.*

Continuing our journey along the French Riviera, the enchanting Villa Santo Sospir stands as a remarkable example of coastal interior design and its integration into the modernist movement. Situated in Saint-Jean-Cap-Ferrat, this gem exhibits captivating decorative interiors adorned with intricate murals that add a touch of magic to its Mediterranean charm. Transformed into an artistic masterpiece by the renowned artist and writer Jean Cocteau (1889–1963), the villa's walls serve as canvases reflecting the sea's allure, mythological tales and the vibrant spirit of the Côte d'Azur. Cocteau's visionary approach blends seamlessly with the coastal surroundings, leaving behind an artistic legacy that stands as testament to the creativity and brilliance of the modernist era.

In 1946, the Villa Santo Sospir found itself under the ownership of the American millionaire Alec Weisweiller and wife, Francine, who intended to celebrate her survival of the World War II with a truly exceptional gift. Known for her effervescent social gatherings, Francine assembled an array of influential guests, including such luminaries as Jean Cocteau, Pablo Picasso, the Agnellis and Yves Saint Laurent. To create a fitting holiday retreat, she enlisted the expertise of internationally renowned interior designer Madeleine Castaing, whose playful and relaxed style added to the welcoming ambiance. With the use of rattan furniture, reeded walls, textured fabrics and white-washed walls, Castaing's design choices exuded a coastal-inspired charm.

However, the true magic was unlocked through the artistic genius of Jean Cocteau, who not only shared a close friendship with Francine but also spent 10 years residing at the villa. Cocteau's remarkable contribution elevated the interiors to the status of a *Monument Historique*. He meticulously transformed the once-plain white walls of Castaing's design into a collection of over 200 linear frescoes. With a masterful hand, Cocteau drew directly onto the walls and incorporated furniture, skilfully using charcoal and coloured pigments mixed with raw

milk to create a mesmerizing tempera that breathed life into mythical tales, evoking a timeless sense of wonder.

The interior became an irresistible allure for celebrities like Coco Chanel, Yves Saint Laurent, Dior and Picasso, who frequently gathered in the captivating dining room. An intricately designed Aubusson tapestry by Cocteau adorned the walls, weaving together a tapestry of art and coastal living over five years. Francine's bedroom, a real sanctuary, featured Cocteau's depiction of a powerful shepherd. Castaing's design of a faux fireplace surround painted in Francine's favourite vivid blue further enriched the vibrant personality of the room.

Through the patronage of Francine Weisweiller, Villa Santo Sospir's extraordinary interiors have become an eternal source of inspiration for successive generations of artists and designers. The whimsical, mythical and coastal essence of these interiors captures the cultural shift toward coastal leisure, perfectly intertwining artistic vision, modernist ideals and the allure of the French Riviera. In this exceptional fusion of creativity and coastal living, the legacy of Villa Santo Sospir stands as an enduring testament to the enchanting impact of coastal interior design along the picturesque shores of the Côte d'Azur.

As we explore coastal interior design, we encounter yet another captivating masterpiece along the French Riviera, the Villa des Troglodytes. Designed by the innovative architect Jacques Couëlle, this extraordinary residence nestles in the picturesque landscape of Roquebrune-Cap-Martin.

Embracing the spirit of the modernist movement, the design seamlessly integrates with its coastal surroundings, forming an organic bond with nature. What sets this villa apart is its unconventional cave-like structure that harmoniously blends with the rocky terrain, further blurring the lines between indoor and outdoor spaces.

left *Whimsical objects on the mantle, recessed bookshelves and the head of Apollo over the drawing room fireplace in the Villa Santo Sospir.*

Inside, a sense of enchantment pervades, as walls curve like gentle waves and straight lines are nowhere to be seen. Couëlle's vision aimed to create a living space that embraced the natural contours of the earth, perfectly encapsulating the essence of coastal living: a harmonious dance with the untamed beauty of sea and land. The design incorporates organic, flowing shapes that mimic the natural colours of the surrounding landscape, further enhancing the villa's integration with its environment.

As with the other coastal architectural wonders we have explored, the Villa des Troglodytes also utilizes local, natural materials such as stone and wood, adding warmth and character to the interior spaces. This approach not only complements the natural setting but also emphasizes the connection between indoor and outdoor spaces. Large windows and open-air terraces invite picturesque views of the Mediterranean to become a part of the interior experience, allowing residents and guests to enjoy the beauty of the surroundings from within.

Drawing from the legacies of Eileen Gray and Jean Cocteau, the villa also prioritizes privacy and tranquillity through its strategic layout and thoughtful design, allowing the occupants to feel both a part of nature and protected from it. Just as Gray and Cocteau incorporated sculptural and artistic elements into their designs, the Villa des Troglodytes also integrates custom artistic elements, adding a sense of individuality and creativity to the space.

Like the other modernist masterpieces along the coast, Villa des Troglodytes features an open-plan layout that fosters a sense of connectivity and allows natural light to permeate throughout the spaces. This continuity with the modernist movement enhances the overall feeling of lightness and openness, once again blurring the boundaries between the indoors and outdoors.

By incorporating the enduring principles of Gray and Cocteau, the villa embodies the very essence of coastal interior design. Its harmonious blend of artistic expression, modernity and coastal living captures the imagination and offers a glimpse into the timeless allure of coastal architecture, where creativity and nature merge to create a truly extraordinary space.

As the sun sets over the glistening waters of the French Riviera, one cannot help but be enthralled by the enduring legacy of coastal interior design. The region has long been a canvas for cultural transformation and artistic expression, where opulent villas of the Belle Époque and modernist masterpieces stand as testament to the spirit of leisure and pleasure embraced by the coastal elite.

opposite *Jacques Couëlle borrows the forms of the natural surroundings in the cave-like interior of his Villa des Troglodytes, similar in its organic approach to the work of Antoni Gaudí's Park Güell.*

The Hamptons

A place of equal enchantment that has captured the imagination of a similar social elite is the Hamptons, an area of startling beauty nestled on the eastern tip of the northern American shores of Long Island. This coastal paradise has attracted seasonal residents and visitors escaping the steamy summers of the East Coast since the 1800s. An area of pristine beaches, rolling dunes, vineyards, farmlands and refreshing ocean and bays surrounding this peninsula explains much of the enduring appeal and the draw for many of the Hamptons' fortunate residents. Around 87 kilometres (54 miles) long and roughly 16 kilometres (10 miles) wide, the peninsula is surrounded on three sides by water, with the Atlantic Ocean on the south curving around Montauk Point to join Gardiners, Napeague and Peconic Bay. This watery setting produces a most magical and unique luminosity much talked about by those in the know, as light dances and glistens from the surrounding sun-dappled waters. Doubtless, this is part of the charm that has drawn artists to these shores since the 1800s.

In the early nineteenth century, these villages and hamlets still reflected the Hamptons of the mid-1600s, when Southampton and East Hampton were first founded as a farming community. In 1640, the original colonists from Massachusetts purchased land from the Shinnecock Indian tribes in exchange for 'Sixty cloth coats, 60 bushels of corn and the promise of military protection'. Today, the agricultural heritage is still present as farmers provide an abundant selection of produce for local grocers, open markets and the many restaurants. This wonderful mix of sea and soil provides a charming backdrop to life in the Hamptons, linking past with present.

right *A shingle-style modern home on the beach in Long Island harks back to the nineteenth-century architecture of McKim, Mead and White.*

The Hampton villages boast their own distinct charm, having retained their maritime and historic architecture. By the eighteenth and nineteenth centuries, whaling was bringing wealth and employment opportunities to the area. Whales were hunted primarily for their oil, which was used for lighting, with demand increasing substantially as cities expanded throughout the 1800s. Whale oil produced a clear, bright light when burned, which provided lighting throughout the expanding states until the late 1800s when advances in the petroleum industry afforded greater and more affordable access to kerosene. Equally, whalebone was valued for its inherent flexibility as this bone, known as 'baleen', could be moulded with heat to form many popular products of the day, acting as a precursor to today's plastic.

The wealthy ship captains returned to their hometowns from whaling expeditions, building impressive Colonial and grand Greek Revival homes, often white-clad with deep blue or green shutters. Many of these remain today along with the docks and former warehouses from this whaling and fishing era, now repurposed into a series of chic boutiques, galleries and eateries. Fortunately, conservation has preserved the unique maritime heritage of the villages with their brick and wooden façades.

Of these architectural legacies, the shingle style has the most iconic and emblematic resonance for those who know the Hamptons. This architectural style is aptly named as these homes were predominately surfaced in shingle. The genius of this material was in the integration of wooden textures, creating harmony and sympathy with the landscape. Equally, the multitude of overlapping angles further softened the exterior façade. This shingle style rejected the more classical architectural precedent of precise symmetry through emphasizing the horizontal planes, which came to represent American architectural freedom as well as relaxed coastal living. With this horizontal emphasis, the layout tended to be asymmetrical with a series of sloping rooflines, expansive porches and equally expansive windows. These expansive porches serve not only as functional outdoor spaces but also as extensions to the interior living areas. They provide a serene vantage point from which to take in the breathtaking Hamptons' landscape, fostering a seamless connection between the indoors and the outdoors.

The prestigious architectural firm McKim, Mead and White built some of the finest examples of this style in the late 1800s. One such example was designed by the notorious partner of the firm, Stanford White (1853–1906). In Montauk, he designed the Seven Sisters, completed in 1884, which stand as a quintessential embodiment of the shingle style in the Hamptons, celebrating the defining factors associated with this architectural legacy. White worked alongside Frederick Law Olmsted (1822–1903), the gifted landscape architect who designed, among other exceptional wonders, Manhattan's Central Park. In Montauk,

Olmsted created a site plan that was sensitive to the natural landscape, linking these seven cottages through meandering pathways and further forging a connection between architecture and nature through linking these habitations, land and sea. The owner was Arthur W. Benson, who commissioned these cottages for himself and a group of friends as a fishing and hunting retreat. Fortunately, these homes still remain today.

Stanford White also designed the Shinnecock Hills Golf Club, located in Southampton, in the same shingled style. Founded in 1892, the club was the first and the oldest purpose-made golf club in the United States, which is so treasured today that it was added to the National Register of Historic Places in 2000. Also noteworthy: the club was the first to admit women from the initial opening, providing a nine-hole ladies' course from 1893.

above *One of the Seven Sisters, the restored DeForest Cottage in Montauk. It was built by McKim, Meade and White and Fredrick Law Olmsted in 1882.*

overleaf left & right *The James L. Breese House, also known as The Orchard, in Southampton was built as a summer residence between 1897 and 1906 by McKim, Mead and White. The home's music room is believed to be Stanford White's last completed project.*

Built on a hill, the clubhouse benefited from cooling breezes, with the entrance facing the ocean on the south side – essential during the summer months in this time before air conditioning. It has also been noted that the location on a hill, near a railway line, popularized the shingle style of architecture, as the Hamptons at that time was still primarily agricultural, with barns and windmills, rather than the cottages of today, visible to those early passengers of the Long Island Railroad.

Shinnecock Hills is also the first golf club to be purpose-built, allowing for enjoyable leisurely relaxation; it is a place to gather and remain, with proper ventilation, comfortable lighting and rooms for lounging. The architect Clifford C. Wendehack (1884–1948) wrote in his book, *Golf and Country Clubs* (1929), that

clubhouses before Shinnecock had 'locker rooms cramped and uncomfortable with insufficient shower accommodations and intolerable ventilation; lounges and dining rooms badly furnished, poor lighting and were generally ill-equipped.'

In Shinnecock, White employed the shingle-style vernacular to wonderful effect to provide generous rooms for an easy flow of people, maximizing light and benefiting from the glorious views and cooling breeze. One of the more revolutionary aspects of the shingle-style interior was a move toward an open and flowing floor plan, away from the more confined, dark and enclosed Victorian architecture and interiors. Other features included high ceilings and substantial and expansive windows, which captured the

seaside and natural beauty of the grounds of Shinnecock, while allowing for improved ventilation and light. In essence, White's architectural choices in Shinnecock were a harmonious blend of aesthetics and functionality, ensuring that club members could fully embrace the splendours of their coastal surroundings.

The club was founded in 1892 by a group of American businessmen, who met Willie Dunn in Biarritz while on their European travels. Dunn (1864–1952) was an English golfer and a golf course designer, who was at that time designing a course in Biarritz. Principal of these investors were William K. Vanderbilt (grandson of Commodore Cornelius Vanderbilt, patriarch of the Vanderbilt dynasty), Edward Meade and Duncan Cryder. These investors were also part of

the New York social society in the late nineteenth century of the elite old families, industrialists and financiers who had the fairly exclusive and privileged access to the coastal region of Long Island and the Hamptons, building lavish summer estates and exclusive social clubs.

For access to Shinnecock and to the spectacular beauty of the Hamptons, it's worth noting that transport in 1892 was considerably more restricted. The Long Island Railroad began service to the Hamptons first on the South Fork of Long Island with completion of the extension to Bridgehampton in 1870, eventually reaching Montauk in 1895. Wealthier families with estates in the Hamptons would often have private carriages, which could be transported with horses by rail or ferry for longer stays.

With this more limited access, the Hamptons remained largely closed to the public, reserved for affluent social elite and those referred to as 'the 400'. This phrase originated from the exclusive guest list of Mrs William Backhouse Astor Jr.'s ball in 1892, to which only the most distinguished of New York society were invited – approximately 400 guests. These wealthy families, including the Astors, the Vanderbilts and the Whitneys, built grand summer estates on Long Island and the Hamptons. The opulent mansions were often referred to as 'cottages' despite their extravagance in both design and scale.

Yet, in addition to these elite summer residents, the artists had arrived as well. Two of whom would become national treasures:

William Merritt Chase (1849–1916) and Winslow Homer (1836–1910). As in the French Riviera, the popularization of the Hamptons for the burgeoning bourgeoisie arose from the invention of the railroad. In the late 1870s, 11 members of the Tile Club, based in New York, were invited by the Long Island Railroad to promote this little-known peninsula. Two of these were Chase and Homer.

opposite & below *The famous 1897 Grey Gardens in East Hampton fell into disrepair under the ownership of Edith Bouvier Beale in the 1970s. Completely restored when bought by* Washington Post *editor Ben Bradlee and his wife in 1979, it underwent another stunning renovation in 2017 when bought by fashion designer Liz Lange.*

William Merritt Chase summered in the Hamptons for over a decade from the early 1890s. For Chase, the pristine sandy beaches and dunes, children at play, brilliant light and ease of outdoor living formed the backdrop for his Impressionist approach to capturing the moment, the impression. Chase often painted *en plein air*, capturing the Hamptons' unique light and scenic landscape. With this approach, he recorded transient moments and atmospheric effects, linking the essence of American Impressionism with the languid pleasures, warmth, light and exceptional seascape of the American coastal beauty.

In 1891, he began teaching art classes in Shinnecock Hills, founding the Shinnecock Summer School of Art. Here, the students engaged deeply with the picturesque national landscape, playing a pivotal role in the development of American landscape painting during this period, with imagery capturing coastal tranquillity and light.

William Merritt Chase also turned to the architect Stanford White, on this occasion for his summer private residence, built in the early 1890s. Situated close to the Shinnecock Summer School, the property was referred to as the Chase Homestead and also as the Pink House due to the distinctive colour. The residence, with its broad porches and sprawling design, captured the essence of the shingle style, affording Chase ample space to paint and teach in addition to providing a comfortable home for his family. With Chase's integration of teaching with his private life, and through the house's proximity to the school, the architecture of Stanford White and the shingle style became a backdrop and architectural reference for budding artists. This further strengthened both the history, scenic landscape and the architecture of the Hamptons with the American aesthetic of the late 1900s.

However, the early twentieth century brought change to the Hamptons as well as to the world at large. After the Great Depression and World War II, many wealthy families faced financial challenges and some estates were converted to other uses or were abandoned altogether. Following these changes at the close of the war, as a growing middle class rose alongside increased automotive ownership, the Hamptons experienced the effects of modernization and suburbanization. Families sought more affordable and generous housing, along with a quieter and safer community beyond the confines of the city. Enhanced transportation infrastructure, such as the highways expansion and the construction of the Montauk Highway, improved accessibility for these ever-increasing motorists, leading to an increase in year-round residents and the growth of suburban communities.

opposite above *The shingle-clad William Merritt Chase Homestead in Shinnecock Hills, circa 1895.*

opposite below *The Shinnecock Hills Golf Club in Southampton is sited between Peconic Bay and the Atlantic Ocean.*

above *The interior of Jackson Pollock's converted barn studio*
(the Pollock-Krasner House and Study Center) in East Hampton.

Equally, the art world moved swiftly away from the landscapes and familial, quotidian scenes of the late nineteenth century. The groundbreaking Armory Show in Manhattan of 1913 marked a shift to modernism and more abstract themes. Unsurprisingly, these trailblazing artists rediscovered the Hamptons. Among the artists was the Abstract Impressionist Jackson Pollock (1912–56). The watery light and eelgrass marshes inspired Pollock when he took refuge in East Hampton with his wife and fellow painter, Lee Krasner, in 1945. With space Manhattan could not provide, Pollock could approach his large canvases from four sides and here perfect his drip technique of painting. In the Hamptons in 1956, he created some of his most iconic and creative works. Today, his shingle-style studio – protected by the Stony Brook Foundation – can be viewed by the public. A guest can enter the studio, observe the light and space and walk upon the floorboards splashed with crimson and yellow, with dashes of lime green, black and sharp ocean shades of blue. In this way, people today can experience the light, air, space and bucolic ease in which the artist created some of his most influential and celebrated paintings.

In the late 1940s and 1950s, Pollock and Krasner formed part of an Abstract Expressionist artists' colony in the Hamptons – all members of the New York School, a term coined in 1949 by the American painter and printmaker Robert Motherwell (1915–91). Members of this movement emphasized non-representational and abstract forms of art, focusing on the emotional and expressive aspects of painting. The leading lights and Hampton residents included Mark Rothko, Willem de Kooning, Franz Kline and Mary Abbott. As artists before them, these pioneering creatives were drawn to the picturesque landscape and serene environment. Though it is strange from our present perspective, they were also lured by the affordable housing costs – all the essential requirements to form a successful artists' community.

left *Willem de Kooning in his light-filled, spacious studio.*

opposite *John Steinbeck, in 1962, on the sun porch of his Sag Harbor home overlooking the waterfront.*

Elaine and Willem de Kooning travelled from Manhattan to East Hampton as guests of Jackson Pollock and Lee Krasner in 1948. In an interview with *Architectural Digest* in January 1982, Elaine said, 'The land, so near the water, and the quality of the light reminded him [De Kooning] of his native Holland.' On land purchased in 1961 not far from the Pollocks in East Hampton, De Kooning built a light-filled studio, with white and glass walls throughout, on a scale he could not recreate in his

Manhattan loft studios. The expansive glass walls allowed the interior to be flooded in sunlight, transforming the studio into a canvas of its own, painting the space with ever-shifting patterns of light and shadow.

In the Hamptons, the writers took refuge too, seeking space, solace and inspiration in the coastal landscape. In 1955 John Steinbeck purchased a waterfront cottage in Sag Harbor, Long Island, which he called 'my little fishing place' and 'Eden'. From the water views over

Morris Cove and Upper Sag Harbor Cove, John Steinbeck wrote his final novel, *The Winter of Our Discontent* (1961), and his 1962 travelogue, *Travels with Charley: In Search of America*. Where the light, space, tranquillity and colours inspired the artists, it is in the towns of this region, their history and the people that inspired Steinbeck's writing. In *The Winter of Our Discontent,* the bucolic and charming town of Sag Harbor was clearly the inspiration for New Baytown. Steinbeck captures the nuances of small-town life with both the history and economic pressures and changes as coastal towns shift from – in this case – a whaling industry to one of tourism.

Sag Harbor was the preferred location for the Sag Main Set, in part due to affordable rent and property prices. The illustrious literary set included Truman Capote, James Jones, George Plimpton and Kurt Vonnegut. A favourite haunt was Bobby Van's. In Bobby Van's, the writers would gather, play games, drink no small amount and cement their literary friendships. One can imagine the freedom these creatives would have felt, away from prying eyes and the busy, confining social scene of New York. Here, they were largely away from people, surrounded by rolling hills with vistas of blue sea, creating a community of their own.

The West Coast

Meanwhile, California, the western coastal frontier, was drawing artists of a different medium, forming another coastal community. As with the artists and writers in the Hamptons of the mid-1900s, actors, as well as producers, directors and writers, flocked to California in search of social freedom from stifling Victorian norms. They were also seeking creative freedom in this new world of Hollywood, as well as freedom of space in the unpopulated golden landscape. The first movie studio emerged in 1911 on Sunset Boulevard and by 1915, many motion-picture companies had relocated from the East Coast. They were drawn to the light and varied landscape of mountains framing glistening, endless shores, though possibly the greatest advantage to those in the industry, who were often filming outside, was the favourable and consistently mild Mediterranean climate. By 1920, the population of Los Angeles had doubled over 10 years. Predictably, the architects followed to provide homes for this growing population, eager to impose their individual and unique mark on the varied landscape. The first part of the 1900s in California was a period of architectural experimentation and groundbreaking development driven by these gifted and imaginative architects. Their creations are naturally worthy of a comprehensive and thorough discussion but for the purpose of our coastal emphasis, here we have focused on two iconic and celebrated residences.

In 1920, Rudolph Schindler (1887–1953) was sent to Los Angeles from Vienna by the iconic architect and designer Frank Lloyd Wright (1867–1959) to supervise construction of the Hollyhock House for the oil heiress, Aline Barnsdall. Schindler's architectural training was steeped in the Viennese Secession movement, having studied with Otto Wagner, a pioneering associate of this movement and celebrated figure in early modern architecture. Wagner, and indeed the movement, taught that modern materials and methods were more relevant and essential than historic references, establishing a forward-

above *A sitting room in a home perched on the coastline of Big Sur, California, with interior design by Mark Boone, who also designed the table and chairs. Through the glass wall is teak outdoor furniture by Michael Taylor Designs.*

overleaf *An exterior view of the Lovell Beach House in Newport Beach, California, designed by architect Rudolf Schindler.*

looking artistic language. Schindler was also largely influenced by the Austrian architect Adolf Loos (1870–1933), who favoured a more organic, individualistic means of designing and experiencing interior spaces. Loos formed the concept he named *raumplan*, a German word that roughly translates to 'plan of spaces'. The raumplan approach prioritizes a three-dimensional interplay of spaces, achieved through a few architectural inventions. This approach allowed for rooms to be arranged in a sequence of varying levels, with each space afforded its own specific height and volume based on function and significance rather than a flat stacking of floors, as in traditional homes. In some instances, a building might have several different ceiling heights on one floor level. These individualized rooms could often interlock or overlook one another, creating complex sightlines. The significance and purpose of this manipulation of volume and size within each room was to create an emotional response to the space. These early modernist architects felt there was a connection to the mental health of the occupant and the rooms they inhabited, which could be manipulated and crafted through careful orchestration of the dimensions and relationship of rooms by rejecting society's conventions and expectations.

The link between architecture and mental and physical health was perfectly suited to Rudolph Schindler's client, Morris Saperstein, who moved to Los Angeles in 1923 and quickly reinvented himself as Dr Philip Lovell to become one of the earliest California health gurus. Lovell was a strong proponent of naturopathy, a form of alternative medicine that emphasizes natural remedies and focuses on the body's innate ability to heal and maintain itself. He was known for his somewhat eccentric health routines, which included sunbathing, vegetarianism, fasting and exercise as critical components of a healthy lifestyle.

Lovell commissioned Richard Schindler to create a coastal home in Newport Beach, the Lovell Beach House. Completed in 1926, this residence is one of the more iconic and representative examples of American modernism. Here, Schindler's humanizing of the house, modern materials and proportion were complemented by Lovell's belief in the home as an essential tool, assisting in his link between coastal lifestyle and wellness. The three-storey structure is notable for its use of a concrete frame and the separation of the living spaces from the ground through the use of pilotis, which are supporting columns. The house literally floats above the parking and garden areas, creating an open-plan outdoor living space beneath the main interior. Employing a key raumplan concept, the interiors were divided into distinct zones, avoiding independent enclosed rooms. This layout allows rooms throughout to benefit from the enormous wall of glass on the western elevation, creating an almost imperceptible break of the interior from the exterior, framing the spectacular view of golden sand and the endless Pacific Ocean stretching to the horizon.

The use of windows throughout allowed for an engaging interplay of light and shadow through the day. Equally, this design provided well-lit and airy interiors, enhancing the connection to this coastal environment. One of the more striking features is the seamless blend of indoor and outdoor spaces. Balconies, terraces and expansive windows provided a connection to the environment, enhancing the dynamic interior layout and flow of spaces.

Here, Schindler was able to employ modern materials with innovative human scale, volume and layering of floor levels, which complemented Lovell's heath objectives. These objectives were perfectly fused with the benefits of coastal living, allowing for both fresh air and warmth. Lovell believed that UV rays through glass allowed a resident to take advantage of sun exposure while still indoors. The Lovell Beach House had an open floor plan, which allowed for natural

above *Built-in furniture in a Lovell Beach House bedroom.*

opposite *The Lovell Beach House is raised above its beach site and supported by five concrete frames. The interior is arranged around a two-storey living and dining area.*

cross-ventilation – the key to Lovell's health principles and teachings. Lovell advocated fresh air circulation to reduce the risk of respiratory diseases. The prominent outdoor terraces and balconies allowed for an abundance of light, while also providing ample locations for sunbathing as well as opportunities to sleep outdoors. The house's multi-levels promoted physical activity. Lastly, the breathtaking views of the Pacific Ocean provided therapeutic and mental health benefits, connecting the happy homeowner to nature and the sense of tranquillity that nature elicits. Lovell wrote, 'When we consider that we spend at least half of each day's hours in the home, the importance of building a structure for health purposes is evident.' In the Lovell Beach House, Rudolph Schindler was able to mix this rich blend of European modernism with a more nature-centric ethos to create a new American and coastal architectural vernacular.

Where Schindler embodied modernism, brothers Charles and Henry Greene advanced the Arts and Crafts movement and ethos. The pair had a profound influence on California architecture and the popularization of this movement, which was also favoured by Frank Lloyd Wright. However, while Wright worked all throughout the United States, the Greene brothers worked exclusively in California. In 1893, they moved from the Midwest to Pasadena. Their primary clients were Midwesterners who wintered in Pasadena and it was there that they forged their reputation, designing every aspect of these Arts and Crafts masterpieces. As with Wright, they sought control over every aspect of a design, from door ironmongery to rugs and lighting, lampshades, seating and built-in furnishings, and the landscape in which the house was situated. No aspect was left uncurated.

In 1916, the writer Daniel L. James commissioned Charles Greene to design an Arts and Crafts residence. Named Seaward, it was perched on a rugged cliff overlooking the dramatic coastline of Carmel. Against this spectacular, theatrical setting, Greene employed the tools of Arts and Crafts design, which included the use of natural materials, exceptional craftsmanship and the integration of the residence into the landscape. Attention was applied to every detail. With locally quarried sandstone and granite, the outer walls appear to grow from and out of the rugged cliff. This integration with nature is one of the greatest triumphs of Seaward, with curved openings along the pathways framing an azure endless ocean view. Here once more, the coastal landscape is seamlessly integrated into the architecture. Greene crafted intricate woodwork and stone carvings depicting the surrounding plant and wildlife, with seaweed, shells and seagulls linking the exterior coastal world. Enormous windows frame the uninterrupted ocean view beyond and arched openings in internal passages and rooms provide a continuous link with westward

opposite *A view from inside Seaward, also known as the D.L. James House, in Carmel-by-the-Sea.*

views. 'California, with its climate, so wonderful in its possibility, is only beginning to be dreamed,' wrote Charles Greene on arrival from the Midwest. Little did he know that he and his brother would elevate and define the American Arts and Crafts aesthetic, forming an iconic California architectural style.

California was essential in crafting and disseminating the vernacular of coastal design. Greene and Greene, like Frank Lloyd Wright, championed Japanese influences in their Arts and Crafts architecture and design. This link continues in coastal decoration. Blurring the lines between indoor and outdoor and open-plan layouts is equally fundamental to Japanese design as well as coastal interior layouts. For the celebrated architects who crafted the early twentieth century California environment, Frank Lloyd Wright, Greene and Greene as well as Rudolph Schindler and the Austrian-American Richard Neutra (1892–1970), this seamless integration of outdoor and indoor spaces was not just a design objective. These architects believed that their innovative architectural theory also improved the creativity, health and emotional wellbeing of the inhabitants.

This vernacular found new and imaginative purveyors in the twentieth century through the emergence of a burgeoning industry, interior design. In 1897, the celebrated novelist Edith Wharton (originator of such classics as *The Age of Innocence* and *The House of Mirth*) joined with architect Ogden Codman Jr. (1863–1951) to co-write *The Decoration of Houses*. Considered to be one of the founding documents of modern interior design, this heralded the beginning of a new era and industry, viewed from the perspective of the interior of a home.

right *Seaward was built by architect Charles Greene using locally quarried stone to appear as if it was growing out of the cliffs. The home was purchased by actor Brad Pitt in 2022.*

Of these, one interior designer emerged to define the coastal language of interiors. Michael Taylor was born in Modesto in 1927 and raised in Santa Rosa, California. His early years were influenced by his grandmother's love of walks in this California landscape, which shaped an interest in the rich and varied coastal environment. With their easy and pared-down elegance, the works of interior design legends Elsie de Wolfe (1859–1950), Frances Adler Elkins (1888–1953) and Syrie Maugham (1879–1955) were particularly influential on the young Taylor. Maugham's White Look of the 1920s was an essential inspiration for Taylor, whose decorative objective was formation of light and airy interiors. He found that white, in its variations of beige, was the perfect tool to create this perception of brightness, bringing the California airy, sun-kissed brightness into the home.

Taylor's individual and inventive interiors are considered standard design tools today but were novel ideas at that time and came to represent the 'California look'. The look was defined by 'white walls, white floors, the perfect plant'. For Taylor, plants prevented 'a room from feeling over-decorated, softened the light and helped a room breathe and feel alive'. It is important to remember that before

Taylor, plants were viewed as appropriate for conservatories and winter gardens alone, not for the main living space. Wicker was another of his innovative and playful tools taken from the exclusive use of outdoor rooms into the primary interiors. Although this was also a tool employed by Madeleine Castaing in the Villa Santo Sospir, it was in Taylor's interiors where the trend was popularized, further blurring the lines between the outer and inner areas by literally importing the outside seating area along with verdant plants and trees into the pivotal domestic interior spaces. These innovative tools further linked the objectives of the early architects of the California design

below *Syrie Maugham's all-white drawing room in her Chelsea home in King's Road, London.*

with Taylor's design intention of 'bringing the outdoors in'. His rooms were filled with exterior materials – furnishings in wicker, windows free of curtains to integrate the exterior and often coastal view, natural materials such as stone floors, organic natural wood forms in furnishings and a multitude of plants in exotic pots. The 'California look' has provided the language for the coastal look. Whether the view captures an azure ocean or a neighbour's garden, these references evoke a feeling of ease and import airy brightness, a sense of wellbeing and tranquillity. Taylor wrote that his intention was 'to combine everything suitable that gives a room the feeling of freshness, originality and a more beautiful atmosphere for living'.

Michael Taylor's coastal interior design bridges the geographical and stylistic gaps between the French Riviera, California and the Hamptons. His unique ability to capture the essence of coastal living in its various forms reflects a universal appreciation for the coastal allure, where artistry and functionality blend to create timeless and captivating interior spaces that pay homage to the beauty of the coast. His work seamlessly encapsulates the charm of the Mediterranean with the relaxed elegance of Southern California and the refined sophistication of the Hamptons. In a world where the coastal lifestyle is universally admired, Taylor's design offers a timeless expression of this enduring fascination.

right *The Beyer House in Malibu, by architect John Lautner, with interiors by Michael Taylor. Organic elements, including boulders, cut stone, trees and wood, were brought inside and blurred the line between the natural world and the home in Taylor's work.*

Beautiful coastal and beachside homes capture the imagination like no other and are an endless source of aspiration and inspiration. The following pages present a celebration of exemplary coastal interiors from around the world, reflecting the different landscapes and locations and including the work of some of the most noted architects and designers in the field.

Along with magnificent interiors of cliff-perched luxury mansions, there are shingle-clad residences and beach cottages. Here you will find expansive open-plan entertaining spaces, as seen in Alicia Keys and Swizz Beatz's Dreamland and examples of the California Look in John Lautner's Carbon Beach House in Malibu and Elie Tahari's home in New York. For more delights, there is the intimate interior of Tom Scheerer's Harbour Island home, as well as the remarkable example of island design that is Veere Grenney's Bamboo Beach House in Mustique. Here you will

showroom

also find inspiration for how the features and themes of coastal design — as outlined in the Elements section of this book — can be incorporated and work together within the architecture of a home.

opposite *This magical interior of a beach house in Cornwall, England, by the renowned architect Alex Michaelis, captures the essence of coastal luminosity by washing every surface in white. The perfect shade to emulate the airy, breezy atmosphere of the seaside, white reflects the natural light so essential to coastal design. Here the play of varied surfaces and the double-height structure accentuate this open space. Light dances on each brilliant surface, bouncing off the satin-painted joinery finish and highlighting the varied white and sandy beige shades of the plaster walls. Even the wood flooring is in the palest hues and the frameless window seamlessly brings the outside in by creating an uninterrupted view.*

left *A.M. Stern Architects and interior designer Steven Gambrel crafted this exceptional shingle-style residence in East Quogue, New York. Wooden planks are synonymous with a relaxed and nautical theme, and import an instant coastal feeling. Wonderfully, the painted planks on the ceiling and walls in seafoam white and varied shades of blue mirror the ocean view beyond, with these shades repeated in the furnishings and bed linen. Cleverly, the designer returns to this theme by repeating the verdant exterior shades in the chandelier, transporting this idyllic coastal panorama into the room's interior.*

overleaf *In this shingle-style residence in Southampton, Charlie Ferrer plays masterfully with the texture and warmth of natural wood on the ceiling, windows and doors. Framing the ocean view with full-height powder blue sheer curtains links the transparent drapery with the ocean beyond, while coastal informality and ease complete the interior through the layered seating arrangements.*

left *This Bridgehampton residence, expertly designed by Stella Architects, captures relaxed coastal informality. Through an edited colour palette of golden yellow hues, verdant seagrasses and beige sands, the interior reflects the coastal world beyond in this artfully crafted mid-century-modern interior. Here the beige tones in the upholstery, walls and ceiling mirror the golden sands of the coastal view, creating an uninterrupted experience. In this curated interior, even the artwork and window are framed similarly in sympathetic tones, transforming the view of the dunes and ocean into artwork.*

overleaf *Natural materials take centre stage in this theatrical interior by HS2 Architecture and interior designer Tom Flynn for Elie Tahari in Sagaponack, New York. Here unfinished beams, fitted joinery, wooden furniture, sisal and rattan produce textural drama and visual warmth. Along with the curated furnishings and a two-storey wall of windows importing the exterior views, this reflects a masterful Hamptons play on the California Look.*

above *Against a cobalt coastline in the idyllic community of Alys Beach, Florida, architect Michael Imber and designer Lynn Myers evoke the essence of resort living. With white-washed walls, arches and sun-bleached wood, the décor draws on exotic vernacular from regions such as Bermuda and Morocco.*

opposite & overleaf *Interior designer Madeline Stuart captures coastal with her layering of textures in her Santa Barbara residence. In the bedroom, she retained the original terracotta tile flooring, a tradition in California Mission-style architecture. In both rooms, wooden planks line the ceilings and walls.*

left *Wallace E. Cunningham designed this modern marvel in La Jolla, San Diego, now owned by Alicia Keys and Swizz Beatz. Known as the Razor House, and now renamed Dreamland, this residence of white cement and frameless floor-to-roof glass seamlessly links the coastal exterior with the interior. The sandy brightness allows the view to take centre stage, with the floor, walls, soft furnishings and even the art in the same cream hue. Organic forms continue this playful, coastal theme, while allowing for a successful seating arrangement in a less traditional room layout.*

overleaf *In this sun-bleached Malibu interior, the ingenious interior designer Kelly Wearstler fills the space with materials found in the coastal landscape. Through driftwood sculptures, organic wooden shapes and the metal re-creation of the palm frond in the ceiling pendant, Wearstler harnesses the natural world. Continuing this theme, the floor-to-ceiling glass doors seemingly remove the architectural barriers to the exterior view, masterfully 'bringing the outdoors in'.*

previous page *Carbon Beach House, the John Lautner residence in Malibu, has been exquisitely restored by architect Michael Kovac and interior designer Waldo Fernandez (for Jamie McCourt). Frameless windows allow the outside to join the interior almost invisibly, while the sumptuous tones in the furnishings unite the wood ceiling and fireplace wall with the view beyond through a colour palette of driftwood taupe, emerald green and sandy shades of beige.*

left *This exquisite room, expertly crafted by KAA Design for a house in Laguna Beach, is a prime example of a seamless fusion between inside and outside. The extension of the wooden slatted roof and textured painted brickwork from the veranda harmoniously connects the room to its coastal environment. The meticulous curation of natural materials, as seen in the jute rug, the heavily textured wooden coffee table and the rattan ottoman cushions, further enhances the quintessential coastal aesthetic, embracing outdoor elements within this interior sanctuary.*

left *Cliff Face House, by Sydney architects Peter Stutchbury and Fergus Scott, uses the architectural vernacular to beautifully frame the coastal view. Aligning the structural buttressing with the glazing panels creates a continuous grid formation, drawing your eye in two directions: towards the coast and upwards, highlighting the impressive scale.*

overleaf *This captivating space in Australia's Bilgola Beach is by Seattle-based Tom Kundig, who installed louvred shutters that fold upwards to expose the space to glorious coastal air and sea views. Kundig's meticulous selection and repetition of key materials culminate in a harmonious and cohesive ambiance. The strategic use of tongue-and-groove panelling on both walls and ceiling creates an authentic coastal backdrop, showcasing the importance of natural materials. To counterbalance the richness of the timber tones, white upholstery has been elegantly employed, introducing a visual and airy contrast on the exquisitely tailored sofa, custom-made to optimize the room's proportions.*

right *In their design for Whale Beach House, Australia, Burley Katon Halliday (BKH) masterfully minimizes their colour palette to just three shades, creating an elegantly restrained interior. They blend warm whites reminiscent of ocean waves with natural rattan tones and bold black accents, resulting in a harmonious and serene ambience. The skilful use of these hues, with playful variations in application, texture and finish, ensures a seamless blend of every element. Additionally, extending the same finish from the balcony to the interior brings the coastal environment indoors.*

opposite *Tom Scheerer's remarkable coastal home on Harbour Island in the Bahamas is a testament to his mastery of coastal interiors. The architecture and interior design artfully harmonize essential coastal elements, effortlessly bridging his interior with the coastal environment, epitomizing the relaxed coastal lifestyle. Skilfully integrating outdoor materials like rattan and wood, in his curated furniture selection, paired with a modernized nautical stripe and the timeless coastal blue and white colour palette, Scheerer elevates the conventional coastal aesthetic, presenting a playful and rejuvenating interpretation. The timber ceiling, juxtaposed against the white walls, gracefully accentuates the remarkable ceiling height, enhancing the breezy ambiance of the coastal setting. The inclusion of coastal objects and indigenous plants further strengthens the seamless connection between the exterior and interior spaces, contributing to a harmonious blend between both.*

overleaf *Veere Grenney, the brilliant mind behind the Bamboo Beach House in Mustique, has astutely chosen a quintessential local material, readily available in the area. By ingeniously omitting visual interruptions, Grenney immerses the user in the all-encompassing ambiance he has masterfully crafted. The playful application of bamboo on every visible surface cleverly camouflages any architectural quirks, infusing the space with a whimsical 'beach folly' charm. By using a single material and visual tone for walls, ceilings, floors and furniture, the only visual interruptions come from the indigenous greens and warm whites, ensuring a seamless harmony with the warm, woody atmosphere. This design retains the unassuming essence of the island, exemplifying how a property's surroundings can authentically influence its interior. It is tailor-made for its idyllic setting.*

right *This beach shack in Oaxaca, Mexico, captures the transformative power of introducing functional design elements within a space and its dynamic impact on the interior. The seamless integration between the expansive wraparound decking and the interior is masterfully elevated through the creative interplay of bi-folding shutters and walls. Treating both movable and solid elements of the structure in the same way creates the illusion of walls effortlessly sliding aside, revealing an uninterrupted connection between the interior and the exterior. This ingenious design approach has magically transformed a humble beach shack into a captivating and visually dynamic coastal hideaway.*

opposite & above *This alluring space was thoughtfully designed by Marina de Lasteyrie du Saillant for her home in Cap Ferret, France. The bright, soft and casual upholstery in the sitting area stands in delightful contrast with the warm and solid saturations of the timber-panelled walls and ceiling. The impeccably tailored corner banquette maximizes the internal space and, by being positioned against the windows, bridges the gap between seascape views and interior comfort. The windows are gracefully framed by rattan roller blinds set at varying levels.*

The entire space of Marina's coastal kitchen is enveloped in wood, embodying the strength and authenticity that such materials can bring to coastal design. The kitchen exudes a relaxed charm with its mix of furniture, featuring a delightful combination of bamboo and rattan chairs alongside a metal-based trestle table. A carpet adorned with rust tones cleverly repeats the warmth of timber to the floor, while playful elements emerge through the tile and woodwork paint finish, adding a touch of coastal whimsy to the overall design.

left *This captivating room in Spetses, Greece, designed by architect Nikos Moustroufis and designer Isabel López-Quesada, beautifully reimagines the classic blue and white palette in a contemporary and unexpected way. Painting both the floor and ceiling blue, while leaving the walls white, enhances the room's brightness, creating a relaxed coastal aesthetic while maintaining the airy ambiance. To amplify the sense of openness, furniture with open frames has been selected, ensuring a continuous flow of space beneath each piece. Accent cushions featuring breaks in the colour palette add a casual touch, and the strategic placement of the daybed creates a focal point for relaxation.*

left & overleaf *Jacques Grange's enchanting Portuguese house in Comporta, designed for collector Florence Grinda, epitomizes rustic refinement. His expert restraint captures the authentic essence of its bohemian surroundings, embracing casual elegance and effortless living.*

Grange has artfully incorporated traditional building materials, such as sun-bleached raw wood, harmonizing the hideaway with its environment. By using the same material on both walls and ceiling but changing the direction, he introduces subtle visual interest. Grange has curated exquisite objects and artifacts from local craftsmen, and the addition of rattan introduces a warmth against the bleached panelling. The continuous white paint unifies the living area, evoking a seaside paradise while paying homage to the traditional cabana architecture of the region.

Despite the eclectic mix of textiles, textures and colours on display, Grange balanced the contrasting warm saturated tones within the bright white interior. Due to Grange's exceptional eye, the objects appear artfully styled rather than cluttered.

Offering decorative inspiration for anyone who lives by the water or simply dreams of doing so, this chapter details the themes, features and key elements that come together to define coastal design. From colour palettes, patterns and materials to lighting, furniture and furnishings, these pages will help you to identify the style and to create a seamless coastal interior of your own.

White on white and blue and white colour schemes achieve a freshness that keeps rooms feeling open and airy, while earthy colours continue the indoor-outdoor narrative, particularly in more tropical interiors, to incorporate tones of driftwood and dunes. Nautical stripes, tropical botanicals and colour blocks can add punch, while tonal whites create a pristine, calm environment. Natural materials, such as rattan and sisal or seagrass flooring, and wood panelling add texture and warmth, as do woven fabrics such as linen and canvas. Floaty sheer

elements

white curtains or pared-back minimal window treatments allow for unobstructed views of the scenery outside, or choose shutters or blinds that are easily adapted to your varying light and temperature requirements. Finally, add personality and charm to your home by decorating with nautical objects and beachcombing finds, such as shells, driftwood and coral, and by bringing the outdoors in with greenery.

opposite *Ocean-wave stone tiles on the floor and walls, mixed with industrial materials and a porthole-style mirror, gives a ship-like feel to a wash room in Kelly Wearstler's Malibu home.*

Blue & White

The quintessential coastal colour combination, blue and white evokes the very essence of seaside living. Blue carries the luminosity of the sea directly into the interior sphere, while white enhances the sublime quality of light that permeates a coastal setting. This colour duo forges a harmonious continuity between indoor and outdoor spaces.

However, it is essential to recognize that the success of this dual-colour equation hinges not only on the choice of colours but also on their specific applications and shades. To steer clear of clichés and create truly timeless coastal interiors, the shade of blue you select is pivotal. The sea's hues are ever-changing, so it's wise to explore the natural tonal variations observed in the ocean rather than, for example, adhering to a stereotypical navy blue.

Shades of Blue

Lighter shades of blue serve a similar purpose to white in that they are gentle on the eye and contribute to a calming, bright and airy ambiance. When you combine these paler blue tones with white, they form a harmonious partnership within the space, creating an instinctive balance. This approach is particularly well-suited for bedroom suites, as it instantly instils a tranquil effect.

When you opt for a predominantly paler colour scheme, especially in reception spaces, there's an opportunity to introduce visual pops of colour that break up a neutral palette and infuse personality into the room. These splashes of colour can be achieved effectively through contrast colour blocks applied through fabrics or furniture, injecting an unexpected quality into the space.

Pattern & Scale

If you desire a more pronounced contrast between the blues and whites, consider employing patterns. Whether through fabrics or wallpaper, patterns allow you to modulate the intensity of the colour contrast, aligning with the degree of impact you wish to achieve.

Smaller patterns offer a subtle approach, allowing the dual colours to be illustrated but in a nuanced manner, creating a refined balance in the space. Conversely, larger patterns pack a significant punch, essentially shaping the personality of the room. By using stronger patterns as the principal design element, you can then layer in solid applications of the blues and whites to maintain visual strength while providing respite from the pattern.

When it comes to layering patterns in your coastal interior, don't be afraid to mix and match within the same space. But do ensure that the scale of these patterns harmonizes with one another. To achieve a visually pleasing result, first consider the focal point of the room. Each pattern competes for attention, and the

opposite *A mix of blue patterns in an interior designed by Andrew Howard in Rose Cottage, a shingled home in Ponte Vedra Beach, Florida.*

dominant pattern will naturally draw the eye first. Therefore, strategically position the dominant pattern in a way that directs visual attention to the room's most significant feature or area, allowing other patterns to complement rather than overpower it. When the scale and placement of patterns are thoughtfully orchestrated, you can layer them with confidence, creating an engaging and dynamic coastal interior while maintaining a cohesive look overall.

These design choices give you the freedom to dictate the mood and character of your coastal space. Whether you opt for subtle colour accents or bold patterns, your design approach will shape the ambiance of the room, ensuring that your coastal interior reflects your unique style.

Coastal Aesthetics

Certain shades of blue and white carry immediate associations with specific countries. The iconic 'Greek' blue, for instance, effortlessly transports one's imagination to the picturesque Greek islands. These islands are renowned for their architectural charm, where vibrant blue accents harmonize with the textured white-washed façades, creating a captivating contrast.

This compelling coastal palette can be seamlessly extended into the interior sphere, as exemplified in this inspiring example. The use of colour blocking, as illustrated here, captures the authentic charm of the Greek islands and translates it into an equally effective interior design. The combination of these distinct blue and white hues lends an air of authenticity and a timeless appeal, evoking the serene beauty of Greece's coastal landscapes.

The iconic hand-painted Delft blue and white tile, synonymous with Portuguese culture, offers a distinctive colour tonality characterized by a more regal blend of royal blue and pristine white.

left *A blue and white interior in Spetses, Greece, mirrors the buildings and landscape outside.*

opposite *Hand-painted Porto design wallpaper by De Gournay, created with Alessandra Branca, as seen in the home of De Gournay designer India Holmes.*

left *Traditional blue and white tiles in a historic Dutch home in a fishing village on what was once the Zuiderzee.*

Its decorative appeal has sparked the creative imagination of successful product developers. One striking example of this reinterpretation is the collaboration between Alessandra Branca and De Gournay, in the form of hand-painted wallpaper. This innovative approach modernizes the traditional tile design by showcasing the beauty and versatility of blue and white in a fresh and contemporary way. This creative adaptation of a classic motif demonstrates the enduring appeal of blue and white, celebrating its ability to transcend traditional boundaries and find new life in the world of interior design, thereby enriching our living spaces with cultural significance and aesthetic delight.

Incorporating evocative coastal colours into your interior design allows you to capture the essence of a specific region and infuse your space with the spirit of a coastal getaway. By embracing the nuanced shades of blue and employing them thoughtfully alongside white, you capture the ever-changing beauty of the sea and infuse your coastal interiors with a timeless, serene and refreshing allure.

White on White

The allure of the coastal setting lies in its luminosity. Therefore, it's a natural instinct to envision a coastal interior painted entirely in white, as a means to capture and harness the radiant essence of the surroundings. This 'all-white' approach creates the brightest space imaginable.

Using a single colour eliminates concerns about colour clashes or pattern coordination within the design. With white, there's virtually no risk of selecting a colour that might darken or shrink the room unintentionally. However, as with most design choices, there's an art to getting it right.

Tonal Whites

White, like any other colour, has a multitude of tonal variations. To avoid a sterile and clinical feel, it's essential to explore these tonal nuances to create visual interest. Warm white tones introduce a relaxed and softer aesthetic, infusing a sense of comfort and ease into the space. Meanwhile, brighter whites layer in drama and impact, providing a striking contrast that elevates the overall design.

By creatively playing with these tonal variations, you can transform your all-white coastal interior into a captivating canvas that balances luminosity, warmth and visual intrigue. It's a design approach that celebrates the inherent brightness of the coast while infusing it with a unique and harmonious character that speaks to the essence of coastal living.

When you opt for a single colour as the backdrop in your coastal interior, there's a certain vulnerability that comes with it. With no colour blocks or decorative patterns to distract the eye, every element within the space becomes more pronounced, and the decisions you make carry greater weight and significance.

However, this inherent simplicity generates a visual strength. By minimizing distractions, a serene and uncluttered environment is created, where each choice and detail can be considered with greater care and intention. In essence, this emulates the design philosophy that celebrates the coastal setting as the main attraction, captivating the eye and evoking a profound connection with the surrounding beauty.

Layering Textures

When working with a single colour palette, the art of layering different textures becomes even more crucial. Within the same space, the same colour can adopt different personalities based on its application and the texture it interacts with.

The colour used can be the same throughout the space, but its appearance varies depending on the surface it's applied to. Wooden beams absorb the paint differently, creating a distinct visual variation and interest as the texture of the timber imparts its own character to the colour.

opposite *A colour palette of whites accented with soft blues in a Nantucket beach house.*

In contrast, the same white paint used on a plastered wall appears as a different tone. It's fresher and brighter, devoid of the timber undertones. This juxtaposition between the two surfaces adds depth and dimension to the room's monochromatic design.

The upholstery also plays a role in this interplay of textures and tones. The subtle tonal changes within the upholstery allow it to seamlessly blend into the space while also contributing its own unique textural qualities.

This skilful layering of textures not only enriches the visual appeal of a room but also underscores the sophistication and depth of the overall design. It's a testament to the power of texture in transforming a single-colour palette into a multidimensional, harmonious and visually captivating interior.

above *Whites and warm natural tones in a Malibu beach house.*
opposite *Accents of citrus orange and lime in a white interior in Bridgehampton.*

Accent Pieces

When you opt for an all-white interior, you're effectively creating a gallery-like setting for your accent pieces, whether they are carefully curated objects or vibrant accent cushions. Within this pristine white backdrop, any item that deviates from the colour scheme will naturally stand out, becoming a focal point in the space. As a result, it becomes crucial to carefully plan the placement and balance of these accent pieces within the room. Their strategic arrangement can transform your interior into a curated exhibition where each piece commands attention and contributes to the overall visual narrative. It's a great way to infuse personality and character into the space while still allowing the coastal view to remain the ultimate centrepiece.

Textiles & Fabrics

In a coastal setting, there's an inherent desire for escapism, and your choice of fabrics plays a pivotal role in creating that relaxed, seaside vibe. Unlike the formality associated with urban dwellings, coastal interiors should lean towards fabrics that exude a casual, carefree charm. Opting for linens and cottons is a wise choice, favouring their breezy, lightweight qualities over heavier, piled options. These fabrics effortlessly extend the easy-going, playful nature of coastal living into your interior spaces, while also considering the surrounding climate.

Materials & Textures

When selecting fabrics, it's crucial to think beyond aesthetics and consider the tactile experience they offer. Particularly in warm coastal climates, where more skin is exposed, the fabric's composition becomes paramount, as it directly interacts with the body. A fabric that feels hot and sticky against the skin can detract from the overall comfort of the space. Hence, practicality must be a significant factor in your selection.

Durability is another vital consideration, and thanks to remarkable advancements in outdoor and recycled fabrics, you can now source materials that are both incredibly robust and soft, akin to traditional indoor textiles. For a coastal setting, especially in high-traffic areas susceptible to beach and sun cream residue, outdoor fabrics are a wise choice. They allow you to embrace lighter colour palettes without the worry of rapid wear and tear. Achieving high performance and luxury in equal measure is the key to a successful coastal interior.

Breezy linens are a perennial favourite in coastal décor. They effortlessly create a relaxed atmosphere and are versatile enough to be used for upholstery, drapery and skirted tables. Beautifully weighted linens are perfect for curtains and can be installed lined or unlined, depending on the desired level of casualness and texture you wish to infuse into your coastal setting.

When it comes to colour, draw inspiration from the coastal setting itself. Consider incorporating hues that pay homage to the natural beauty of the area — think the vibrant or subtle blues of the ocean, the gentle coral pinks found in seashells or the radiant sunshine yellows reminiscent of a coastal sunrise. By infusing these colours into your fabric choices, you allow the very essence of the seaside to flow into your interior, amplifying the sense of airiness and lightness that coastal spaces are renowned for.

opposite *Delicate canopy curtains with a detailed quilt bed cover offers rest and comfort in a loft bedroom in Tom Scheerer's Harbour Island, Bahamas, home, nicknamed the Cash Box.*

Patterns & Stripes

Patterns in coastal fabrics can be another powerful tool to infuse character and evoke the spirit of the seaside within your interior space. The choice of pattern should mirror the beauty and tranquillity of the coast, inviting a sense of relaxation and escapism.

- Nautical stripes are a timeless choice and their classic appeal harks back to maritime traditions and the soothing rhythm of ocean waves. These stripes, often in shades of blue and white, bring a sense of order and calm to the space.

- Coral motifs or sea life designs evoke the underwater world. Whether delicate coral branches, seashells or playful fish patterns, these prints connect your interior to the vibrant marine ecosystems, adding a touch of whimsy.

- Botanical prints capture the lush greenery of coastal environments beautifully. Think palm leaves, tropical flora or seagrass patterns. These prints introduce a tropical element, making you feel like you're in a beachside paradise.

- Ropes and knots add a charming maritime touch. They symbolize the connection to the sea, and their intricate designs can be both visually captivating and comforting.

- Scenic coastal landscapes, from serene beach scenes to coastal towns and lighthouses, transport you to a specific location, enhancing the overall narrative and sense of place within your interior.

- Soft gradients and watercolour patterns mimic the fluidity of water, giving fabrics a dreamy and serene quality. These patterns create a calming atmosphere, as if you're gazing at the ocean's horizon.

- Geometric patterns that draw inspiration from elements like shells, waves or driftwood infuse a contemporary, beachy vibe into the space, combining tradition with a modern twist.

Incorporating coastal patterns into your fabrics is a way to tell a visual story of the sea and its surroundings. The patterns not only add visual interest but also serve as a reminder of the natural beauty, creating an environment that invites relaxation and a deep connection with the coastal lifestyle.

opposite *Botanical prints in a room at the Tropical Hotel in St Barth, Caribbean, designed by Oscar Lucien Ono, using Mauritius fabric by Pierre Frey in custom colours.*

Rattan

Bringing 'the outdoors in' is a technique employed by designers and architects since the early days of coastal interior design. One way to do this is using rattan furnishings, which bring the warmth and coastal ease into the home. It is a method favoured by Michael Taylor, becoming a pivotal feature of his California Look.

Installing furniture reserved largely for conservatories and garden rooms into the main house is, in itself, a playful gesture. Rattan harnesses the lightness and gaiety of summer days both in the colouration, from the blending and weaving of this natural material, and in the open fretwork and airy structure of the frames themselves. These shapes can vary depending on purpose. Exaggerated shapes like the vintage Emmanuelle Peacock chair are almost artistic statements with their swoopy curvilinear backs. These forms are whimsical and add a lightness into a room's décor.

Rattan shapes can be individual statements, with the furniture, frames or accessories having a personality of their own with clever curves, shapes and forms. They can be sculptural in nature or provide consistency in design. For example, a rattan chair can make an individual statement piece on its own. Or when used as a suite, filled with plush upholstery for a clever spin of the more traditional upholstered seating plan, rattan can pull together a room.

Fabrics too are a place for individuality to use on rattan seating. Use a splash of colour in coral or a pattern on more elaborate wickerwork. Equally, fabric in shades of blue and white are coastal references which return the spirit and mind to the feeling of warmth, golden sun and sand.

right *A vintage rattan chair and table pair with built-in banquette seating in a dining nook in a Fire Island, New York, home.*

above *One of the most well-known elements of coastal design: a rattan Peacock chair.*

opposite *Rattan lights and furniture at the Tropical Hotel in St Barth, Caribbean.*

Rattan Pieces

Rattan has flexibility and strength that provides an excellent natural material for sculptural shapes and delicate frameworks that allow light and air to pass through the design. Light, air, playfulness and golden natural materials are all components of coastal design and found in this varied and sculptural material. There are many styles to add this coastal narrative, whether side tables, bedside tables, pendants, table lamps, consoles, commodes or seating.

- Pendants are a fun and playful means of adding coastal informality to a room. They cast intricate and delicate patterns through a flattering play of light and shadow. Standing lights are also available with frames wrapped in rattan, a welcome change from the more expected materials of metal or wood.

- Mirrors provide whimsical lightness and fun both in design and structure. French Riviera rattan mirrors designed in the 1960s and '70s from designers such as Franco Albini are wonderful examples of this aesthetic. Adding this curvilinear design above a curved rattan commode could create a joyous bar setting for festive summer evenings.

Sisal, Seagrass & Other Natural Materials

Natural materials such as sisal, jute, coir, seagrass and rush add an instant beach vibe to an interior. Here, once again, there is the whimsical play of outdoor materials used indoors. As with rattan, the colour and tonality of the material captures the warmth of a summer day through their golden variegated hues.

Even more relevant today, these renewable resources are both eco-friendly and sustainable, offering some level of insulation. They also provide carbon sequestration during the plant growth and even, in the case of seagrass, support other ecosystems such as mangroves and coral reefs. If the product has been produced in an equally sustainable manner, these materials offer wonderful ways to respect and protect the coastal environment.

right *A Montauk house, designed by Bates Masi Architects, features an earthy colour palette, natural wood and a seagrass rug.*

Flooring & Furnishings

The most popular way to integrate natural materials into an interior is via flooring. The texture, tonality and warmth add an immediate link to the outdoor environment, creating a sensorial experience in ways beyond sight. There is a reminiscence of summer with walks outside, as they mimic the effect of varying terrain and material on bare feet. Often these materials are overlaid with a softer rug in seating areas, where a bit of comfort is desired in more intimate seating groups. Seagrass in particular can introduce an earthy scent, which is not present in the other materials and fades with time. Each material offers differences in feel and effect, but all equally imbue a sense of informality and relaxed chic.

As with rattan, these materials are found in interesting designs for lamps, pendants and furnishings. They add a similar playfulness to a home interior, bringing plant-based and exterior materials to replace fully furnished upholstery. These materials are more solid and less open-weave structures than rattan and provide a different textural effect, which can be mixed with soft upholstery or even rattan successfully. In these furnishings, there can be a variation in gloss or lacquer finish and it is in the less adorned and more unlacquered state that these materials most effectively inhabit the coastal ambience.

Decorative Items

Smaller items, such as log and shopping baskets in varying sizes, can also bring this look into the home. Whether a basket for summer shopping set casually by the entry, a selection of hats on display for protection from the sun's rays or multiple layering of furnishings and lighting, these natural materials add that essence of summer and casual ease.

opposite *A natural seagrass rug unites a trio of rattan furniture to create a welcoming sitting area.*

Tiles

Tiles offer a versatile and functional solution that harmonizes with the natural surroundings and adds a touch of coastal charm to the space. Since coastal living often involves sandy feet and the occasional splash of water, tiles, whether used on floors or walls, are an excellent choice due to their durability and easy maintenance.

The use of tiles allows for endless creative possibilities, encompassing different options in colour, texture and intricate patterns. Through thoughtful selection and application, you can instantly transform a space. For instance, incorporating vibrant, patterned floor tiles can inject a sense of playfulness and character into a room. In this case, make your tile selection a focal point within the design development phase. Then, based on the impact you want to create, you can craft the rest of the design scheme ensuring a harmonious colour balance throughout the room. This approach allows you to achieve a cohesive and visually captivating coastal interior that highlights the inherent beauty of tiles as a central design feature.

In high-functioning spaces, an effective design choice is to fully clad walls in tiles, extending from floor to ceiling. By employing a repetitive motif, these tiles can achieve a visual impact akin to that of patterned wallpaper, while simultaneously introducing texture and durability to the space. This approach proves particularly successful in areas like kitchens, where the practicality of tiles harmonizes seamlessly with the demand for a visually engaging and enduring design solution.

Cultural Influences

If your preference leans towards a high level of ornamentation and a decorative use of tiles, you'll discover a wealth of inspiration from diverse cultures around the world. This traditional approach to tile design is renowned for its intricate and ornate use of patterns, typically incorporating a blend of geometric designs, floral motifs, calligraphy and figurative elements, depending on its origin. This intricate use of tiles elevates the material to an art form, allowing the tile itself to take centre stage as the primary focal point within the room.

opposite *Patterned floor tiles create a focal point and provide a colour palette for a rustic kitchen.*

Accent Tiles

If you aim to use tiles as a balancing element within a space without committing to covering the entire room or floor, you can introduce them as accent features. For instance, in coastal kitchens and bathrooms, tiles are frequently employed as backsplashes or decorative design features. These applications not only shield the walls from moisture but also serve as a decorative element in the room. A backsplash adorned with beach-inspired colours or a traditional applied mosaic can infuse a delightful coastal touch.

opposite *Pale blue and white tiles are matched with royal blue and white in a Bahamas home.*

above *Blue and white tiles evoke a Moroccan hammam in a nook designed by jewellery designer Monica Vinader for her home in Norfolk, England.*

Wood

What could be more representative of bringing the outdoors in than an organic form from a tree trunk for the top of a coffee table or console. These techniques were part of the California Look of Michael Taylor, where at times a crane was needed to lift the element into a room. While this level of complication is probably beyond average means, an authentic way to import the coastal aesthetic into an interior is to choose furniture that represents the natural shape and growth pattern of a tree and that is truly original and authentic. Sculptural wood forms are also available in lamps and wall sconces that often simulate the driftwood sculptural shapes found on coastal shores.

Panelling

The use of wood planks on walls or tongue and groove painted wood panelling is quintessentially coastal. If you are on a budget, there are wallpapers that realistically represent wood graining in a range of shades, and can create a wonderfully realistic impression. MDF (medium-density fibreboard) is another low-cost material that can create the impression of painted wood planks. The texture and warmth of wood in the architectural framework, even as a reproduction, creates the effect of a beach house.

Ceilings should never be ignored, and they offer an unexpected location to showcase the warmth and lustre of wood. Walls can then remain white for a modern aesthetic in a main interior, or for an open and brighter feeling in a tighter space like a passageway. Another successful approach is to use different shades of wood in different directions, one for the walls and the other for the ceiling. For a more traditional and comforting room, the same wood can be used on the walls throughout.

opposite *An eco cottage in Esther's Island, Nantucket. The wood interior incorporates wood studs and weathered shingles that once lined the covered porch.*

Trellising

Another outdoor architectural language imported into interiors is trellising. Traditionally for gardens to aid the growth of climbing plants, this structure has found its way into interiors, on walls, ceilings, doors and cabinetry door faces. Trellis can be used as a door to divide rooms, allowing for light and air to pass between them. Trellis doors can equally integrate two rooms while providing a visual separation. Trellis open fretwork design, even when fixed to a solid door panel, represents this coastal vernacular in that it adds a playfulness, lightness and an outdoor feeling into the home. Even though painted, this addition is a wonderful means of bringing the outside into the home in a whimsical and original manner.

opposite *A window is covered by a simple canvas blind while trellis walls allow air to circulate through the house.*

below *White trellising allows ventilation while maintaining privacy in a Caribbean home.*

Nautical Themes

Nautical themes and coastal imagery can range from small statements to expansive gestures. In the interior, walls offer an ideal landscape for showcasing artwork, wallpaper and oceanic elements applied in a collage, while shelves can display found objects such as shells and coral. A marine-themed painting or modern interpretive landscape that emulates the coastal calm and serenity through colouration and brushwork can impart a sense of peace and wellbeing.

Objects & Shapes

Although shells can seem obvious and expected, they can be used in playful and clever ways to embellish a room. The most successful use is through the unexpected and the larger in scale, such as with decorated mirror frames and furniture or walls covered in shells like a jewel box. Smaller gestures can be wonderful too, and certain shell shapes and coral create superb sculptural contours.

Equally, a collection of shells or cerulean sea glass, housed in matching decorative glass cannisters, can be visually eye-catching. There are enchanting nautical examples that can capture the coastal vibe, even a sailboat ornament or driftwood piece, which when balanced with the coastal elements can recreate the restorative languor in the home. These collections are even more delightful when they represent an individual's or a family's journeys and memories.

Lighting

Lighting offers some delightful options, with lamps, pendants or wall lights either adorned in shells or cast in plaster representing shells with their disparate forms. In the appropriate context, nautical themed lights representing sail boats and sailing elements can be whimsical and witty. Equally, foliage lighting, depicting leaves and fronds, adds charm.

Wallpaper

For even larger impact, wallpaper provides another means of importing a nautical theme. In our work, we have been fortunate to design with De Gournay, who have launched three coastal wallpapers. One depicts a panoramic view of Nantucket Harbor and the Sound, featuring ships, dolphins, whales and white-capped waves. The others include a lovely palette of floating sea creatures and swimming shoals. Papering a room entirely in a nautical theme is truly transportive.

Large palm and banana leaf wallpapers favoured in the 1940s are once more finding an audience, bringing the outdoors in with a tropical verdant theme. Two classics are Dorothy Draper's Jungle Leaf for the Quitandinha in Brazil and Don Loper's Martinique, a large banana leaf for the Beverly Hills Hotel. Both papers are still available for purchase today, and there are many designs and suppliers on the market playing with this theme in a variation of colours and scale.

previous page *Nautical detailing in a children's bedroom in Martha's Vineyard.*

opposite *A hand-painted Nantucket Crossing panoramic wallpaper by De Gournay.*

above *Martinique, a banana leaf wallpaper, by CW Stockwell.*

opposite *Marine memorabilia displayed on a beach house wall in France.*

above *Salvaged buoys are displayed in a panelled entrance hall in a Nantucket beach house.*

Window & Ceiling Treatments

The allure of coastal living is undoubtedly intertwined with the abundant natural light it offers. Coastal architecture pays homage to this luminous quality by celebrating expansive windows and embracing terraces that seamlessly bridge the gap between indoor and outdoor spaces, captivating the seaside vistas that stretch beyond.

In this context, the treatment of windows becomes a point of thoughtful consideration. When the primary goal is to highlight the breathtaking panoramas, the idea of adding curtains or blinds to the windows may seem contradictory.

At the coast, where the primary draw lies in the limitless ocean views, a space can maintain a sense of completeness even without window coverings. The window frames can act as a picture frame, displaying the breathtaking views like works of art and allowing the interior to act as a staging area for the setting beyond.

Pared-back & Bare

If you are inclined towards the minimalist approach of leaving your windows uncovered, introduce alternative elements that infuse visual interest into the space. Window treatments inherently contribute a textural quality and softness to a room. Therefore, you must ensure that this missing dimension is compensated for in other ways.

In this scenario, every surface within the room warrants thoughtful consideration, and this can extend to the often-overlooked ceiling.

Ceilings have, over time, become an afterthought in design, typically receiving a standard white paint treatment out of habit. However, we would recommend assigning the ceiling equal importance in your design scheme, making it an integral part of the immersive experience from floor to ceiling. Achieving this effect can be as simple as incorporating wallpaper, opting for glossy or matte paint, or, in keeping with the coastal theme, using wood to add warmth and character. Through the use of wood, you can channel the lined nature of the grain or planks towards the window, once again drawing your eye towards the captivating coast.

Shutters

When thoughtfully integrated, wooden shutters bring a distinct character that resonates with the coastal aesthetic. Their natural wood grain, when left exposed or subtly finished, carries a sense of rustic charm and authenticity that aligns harmoniously with coastal design principles. The wood's warm, earthy tones evoke the sandy beaches and driftwood often found along the coast, forging an immediate connection to the natural surroundings.

opposite *Minimally dressed windows allow an expansive view of the Noyack Bay from Bay House, located on a bluff in Southampton.*

opposite *White folding shutters connect indoor and outdoor spaces in this beachside house, letting in air and light.*

left *Rolled blinds are positioned further down the windows to control the amount of light without obstructing the view to the outdoors.*

Blinds

In the realm of more private spaces, where discretion and protection from curious onlookers are essential, the need for window dressings becomes apparent. This presents an ideal chance to incorporate a richer tapestry of natural materials. Among these, Abacá, a plant fibre known for its remarkable versatility and innate elegance, stands out as an excellent choice. Not only does it boast sustainability credentials, but it also thrives in humid environments, making it particularly well suited for coastal settings. Abacá can be handwoven into exquisite blinds, effortlessly serving the dual purpose of providing privacy and allowing gentle, filtered light to permeate the space.

Position the blinds as close to the ceiling as possible, so that the blinds discreetly retreat into the upper space. This clever placement ensures that the blind stacks above the window rather than in front of it. By adopting this method, you can enjoy the practical benefits of the blind – such as light control and privacy – without compromising a breathtaking view or impeding the flow of natural light.

Sheer Treatments

If the tactile nature of natural materials doesn't align with your aesthetic, an elegant sheer blind can be just as effective in providing shade and privacy. Hold the sheer fabric up to the light, ideally within the intended space, to assess the intricate details of the thread composition within the fabric. This step is essential to ensure that the chosen material perfectly encapsulates your envisioned aesthetic. You'd be pleasantly surprised by the array of options available in the market and how dramatically the fabric comes to life when bathed in the gentle, coastal sunlight.

Sheer curtains, more so than sheer blinds, have a unique ability to accentuate the coastal ambiance, particularly the refreshing breeze. When billowing gently in the wind, they bring a sense of lightness and airiness to a space. These ethereal curtains serve as a soft, delicate barrier between inside and outside.

Window Design

For those fortunate enough to embark on designing a new coastal home, you have an opportunity to craft a truly unique visual experience when considering the window design, especially in connection with the ceiling. By letting the window shapes interact harmoniously with the ceiling's contours, an exhilarating interplay of shapes and lines can be created and serve as an energized framework within the interior. This dynamic interplay becomes an artistic focal point, amplifying the allure of the coastal panorama beyond and removing the need for window treatments completely.

Such an approach doesn't merely frame the view; it actively engages with it, drawing the eye towards the ever-changing coastal landscape. It's a design philosophy that invites the outdoor beauty into your home, transforming it into a living work of art where the interplay of architecture and nature is in constant, captivating dialogue.

opposite *Sheer curtains billow in the sea breeze that filters in from the beach and flows throughout the house.*

Plants

The home of the American doyenne of design, Rose Tarlow, graced the pages of *Architectural Digest* in June 1991, with vines growing inside the enviably lofty interiors of her California residence, decorating the walls like a three-dimensional fresco. The effect was and is still enchanting. There is little surprise that Tarlow was at ease and fluent in her ability to link plants into her interiors, having embraced and later come to represent California taste. In this case she is aligned with her friend and mentor Michael Taylor, whom Tarlow refers to as 'a genius'. Adding these living verdant forms in an interior imports a relaxed, informal elegance.

There are additional benefits too. It has been proven that indoor plants improve mood, reduce stress levels and foster a sense of wellbeing. This is delightfully aligned with the health intentions and benefits of coastal living. It is a marvellously easy trick to be able to mix both coastal design flair with the coastal objective of greater health and general wellbeing through a trip to the garden centre, without requiring construction or much advanced planning.

right *Palm trees and plants decorate a sunroom overlooking the Mustique coastline.*

overleaf left *For a layered look, combine botanical wallpaper with real houseplants or flowers, as styled here by Summer Thornton. The wallpaper is Palm Jungle by Cole and Son.*

overleaf right *A grand entrance is created with a pair of large tropical plants in an East Hampton home.*

Plant Containers

Another means of adding two compatible and whimsical coastal, indoor-outdoor themes is through integrating containers made of rush or another natural material. The shape and style of these containers, as with the plant selection, is determined by the intended location in the room. Making sure that the light in the room is adequate for the plant to flourish is essential to its vitality and should inform the plant species selected. Interior designers select according to scale, often preferring taller trees with rounded sculptural leaves or fronds, as they create a joyful pattern in the room and produce shapes with the natural play of light and shadow.

Also, there is rarely a room that cannot be improved by the verdant variations of greens available. These glorious living elements are a gift to an interior, mixing their rich, variegated and vibrant colouration with sculptural forms, pulling the beauty of our outer world into the home.

index

ABOUT THE AUTHORS

Jena Quinn and Lucy Derbyshire are the creative minds behind the interior architecture firm Studio QD, a name synonymous with excellence within interior design. As industry innovators, their journey is a testament to their unwavering commitment to crafting remarkable interior spaces, driven by their profound passion for design.

Jena Quinn, a graduate of Parsons School of Design, embarked on her artistic journey following a BA in Art History from UCLA. On the other side of the Atlantic, Lucy Derbyshire earned her MA degree in Art History at St Andrews University. This distinctive fusion of American and British heritage forms the foundation of their collaborative brilliance, honed over decades in the world of interior design.

Jena and Lucy possess an artistic and architectural academic grounding and deep reverence for design spanning the ages. Yet it was in their youth that a passion for coastal living began, for Jena raised on the coast in southern California, and Lucy with her family home on the Algarve coast of Portugal. *Coastal* provided the perfect conduit for blending this lifelong love and attraction to coastal living with their interior design expertise.

See more at: http://studio-qd.com

ACKNOWLEDGEMENTS

Jena Quinn and Lucy Derbyshire would like to thank:
Karen Howes of Interior Archive for her genius and artfully curated visual library
Lisa Dyer for her calm and patient brilliance and expertise
Isabel Bass for her constant beloved friendship and support
Our families for their unwavering support and love.

PICTURE CREDITS

Cover images: ©Tim Street-Porter (front); ©Annie Schlechter/Interior Archive (back)

First published in 2024 by OH
An Imprint of HEADLINE PUBLISHING GROUP

13 5 7 9 10 8 6 4 2

Cataloguing in Publication Data is available from the British Library

Hardback ISBN 978-1-83861-217-7

Printed and bound in China

HEADLINE PUBLISHING GROUP
An Hachette UK Company
Carmelite House
50 Victoria Embankment
London EC4Y 0DZ

OH Publisher: Lisa Dyer
Desk editor: Matt Tomlinson
Design: Lucy Palmer
Production: Arlene Lestrade

www.headline.co.uk
www.hachette.co.uk

ACKNOWLEDGEMENTS

Jena Quinn and Lucy Derbyshire would like to thank:
Karen Howes of Interior Archive for her genius and artfully curated visual library
Lisa Dyer for her calm and patient brilliance and expertise
Isabel Bass for her constant beloved friendship and support
Our families for their unwavering support and love.

PICTURE CREDITS

The publishers would like to thank the following for their kind permission to reproduce the images in this book.

Alamy agefotostock 27; Alpha Stock 42, 43; anutr tosirikul 126; Arcaid 9; Art Kowalsky 12–3; Associated Press 47b; Cinematic 44; Eye Ubiquitous 54; Gina Rodgers 115; Hemis 15, 30–1, 32, 34–5; Mr Megapixel 19; The History Collection 47t. **Alexander Vertikoff** 60–1. **AKG Images** Daniel Frasnay 50; Erich Lessing 10–1; Lothar M Peter 20, 23, 24, 25, 28. **Allesandra Barlassina/@gucki.it** 48–9. **Bridgeman Images** Look and Learn 63. **Christophe Coënon** 37. **CW Stockwell** 143 (photography by Matt Sartain). **De Gournay** 114, 142 (photography by Alexandra Shamis). **Didier Delmas** 122, 127l, 127r. **Getty Images** Canovas Alvaro 104–5, 106–7; John Swope 16–7; Kris Connor 45; Newsday LLC 51; Pgiam 6–7; Print Collector 62. **Gluckman Tang Architects** David Taber 41. **Interior Archive** Annie Schlechter 2 (Barrie Benson), 72–3 (Anna Molvik), 118 (Anna Molvik), 124–5 (Karin Lidbeck), 134 (Liz Strong), 137 (Olga Naiman), 141 (Tracey Overstrand Stead / Liz Strong), 149 (Lynn Morgan), 154 (Summer Thornton); Derry Moore 139 (Oliver Messel), 152–3 (Oliver Messel); Fritz von der Schulenburg 119 (Barefoot Elegance); Jacques Dirand 138 (Oscar de la Renta); Luke White/Perfect Neutrals 155 (Larry Laslo); Mark Luscombe-Whyte 135 (Monica Vinader); Nat Rea 116 (Donna Elle), 145 (Donna Elle); Nicolas Matheus 148, 151; Nicolas Tosi 144 (Monique Duveau); Simon Upton 133 (Peter Benson Miller); Stefano Scata 130 (Rita Polese Salvador); Tim Beddow 67 (Architect: Alex Michaelis). **Library of Congress** Historic American Buildings Survey 56, 57. **OTTO** Eric Piasecki 68–9 (designed by Steven Gambrel and RAMSA), 74–5 (designed by Tom Flynn); Francesco Lagnese 94–5 (designed by Tom Scheerer), 111 (designed by Andrew Howard), 121 (designed by Tom Scheerer); Frank Frances 80–1 (designed by Wallace E. Cunningham); Roger Davies 84–5 (designed by John Lautner); 86–7 (designed by KAA Designs/Atelier AM); Stephen Kent Johnson (designed by Charlie Ferrer) 70–1. **Richard Powers** 76, 77, 78–9, 82–3, 88–9, 92–3, 98–9, 100, 101, 102–3, 109, 112–3, 128–9, 147. **Rory Gardiner** 90–1. **Shutterstock** Durston Saylor/Condé Nast 4–5; Joao Paulo V Tinoco 38–9; Mary E Nichols/Condé Nast 52–3. **Tim Street-Porter** 64–5. **Unsplash** Jon Tyson 59. **Veere Grenney Associates** (photographed by David Oliver) 96–7.

Copyright © 2024 Studio QD
The right of Studio QD to be identified as the Author of
the Work has been asserted by them in accordance with the
Copyright, Designs and Patents Act 1988.

Cover images: ©Tim Street-Porter (front); ©Annie Schlechter/Interior Archive (back)

First published in 2024 by OH
An Imprint of HEADLINE PUBLISHING GROUP

1 3 5 7 9 10 8 6 4 2

Cataloguing in Publication Data is available from the British Library

Hardback ISBN 978-1-83861-217-7

Printed and bound in China

HEADLINE PUBLISHING GROUP
An Hachette UK Company
Carmelite House
50 Victoria Embankment
London EC4Y 0DZ

OH Publisher: Lisa Dyer
Desk editor: Matt Tomlinson
Design: Lucy Palmer
Production: Arlene Lestrade

www.headline.co.uk
www.hachette.co.uk